• WILD GUIDE

TURTLES

Charles Fergus

illustrations by Emily Damstra

STACKPOLE
BOOKS

0 11557 03420 2

Published by
STACKPOLE BOOKS
5067 Ritter Road
Mechanicsburg, PA 17055
www.stackpolebooks.com

Printed in China

10 9 8 7 6 5 4 3 2 1

First edition

Cover design by Caroline Stover
Cover illustration by Emily Damstra
Illustrations by Emily Damstra
Photo credits: Bill Beatty: 64, 94, 104, 106; Gerry Lemmo: 80, 92; Dan Nedrelo: 22, 70,
74, 78, 82, 86, 88, 96; Allen Blake Sheldon: 18, 41, 61, 66, 68, 72, 76, 84,
90, 100, 102; Larry West: 98

Library of Congress Cataloging-in-Publication Data

Fergus, Charles.
    Turtles / Charles Fergus. — 1st ed.
        p.   cm. — (Wild guide)
    ISBN-13: 978-0-8117-3420-2
    ISBN-10: 0-8117-3420-X
    1. Turtles.   I. Title.
QL666.C5F43   2007
597.92—dc22

                                                                                2006031953

CONTENTS

INTRODUCTION

*I look at this turtle in my hand and wonder
what grace allows me to hold and ponder such
a tangible piece of the history of life on earth.*

—David M. Carroll

It was a humid summer day at Pine Ridge State Forest Natural Area in south-central Pennsylvania. Hiking along a trail, I met a wood turtle. It seemed the turtle had seen me first—or had otherwise sensed my presence—for it had withdrawn its head, legs, and tail inside its shell. Its soot-colored face peered out from beneath the protecting carapace.

I sat down beside the turtle; I had plenty of time, and I decided to spend some of it with the reptile.

Over the next five minutes, the turtle extended its head out of its shell, millimeter by millimeter. Reddish orange markings showed on the turtle's neck. The turtle fixed its dark, shiny eye on me. I wondered what the eye saw, and I wondered what the turtle thought about what its eye registered.

Typical for its species, the wood turtle had a beautiful and intricate upper shell composed of raised, pyramidal plates. The shell was a rich dusky brown; darker radiating lines marked each plate, of which there were thirty-eight knit tightly together. Each plate, or scute, was made up of a series of concentric quadrangles, much like the elevation lines on a topographic map. Each line signified a year's growth. When I got my face down near one of the scutes— an approach that caused the turtle to quickly retract its head again—I could make out approximately twenty-five growth lines. Twenty-five years; a quarter of a century. That's a generous life span for a wild animal. Even the larger mammals, such as deer and bears, rarely live longer than ten or a dozen years. And a wood turtle can live to be older than that: Wild ones have survived more than thirty-three years, and captives have lived beyond fifty.

This wood turtle was about 8 inches long by 5 inches wide. On each side of its shell, around the middle part of the carapace, the shell was worn smooth, probably from the turtle pushing itself through weeds and brush. Taking the shell in my hand, I lifted the turtle. In contrast with its earth-colored carapace, the bottom of the turtle's shell—the part known as the plastron—was a rich straw yellow with mahogany black blotches.

I set the turtle back down.

After some time, the turtle put its head out again. It partially extended its limbs; like the head and neck, these also had reddish orange markings, and they were tipped with sturdy black claws. The turtle did not walk off. It continued to stare at me, or at least to stare in my general direction. Edward Hoagland once wrote: "Turtles are a kind of bird with the governor turned low." More time passed. I found myself listening to birds calling, insects buzzing, and the breeze whispering through the crowns of the forest trees. At times I would forget about the turtle sitting next to me. Then I would come back to myself and look at the turtle again. It didn't move. At one point, I realized I was becoming impatient for the turtle to do something. To do anything. The loose skin sheathing the creature's neck pulsed faintly. A fly landed on the slatey, flat-topped head. After a few minutes, the fly walked across the turtle's eye. At which point the turtle actually blinked. When I'd first sat down, the sun had been directly overhead. Now the trees cast shadows across the path. I got up, stretched, and brushed the dust off my pants. The turtle reposed in the same spot where I had put it down after examining its plastron. It stayed there as I walked down the trail.

The turtle, of course, did not exist to entertain or to please me. It did not grasp the concept of "pleasing" anybody or anything, except perhaps its own reptilian self. Yet in its placid, unassuming manner of existing—of simply being—it had done just that. It had sent me a subtle message, telling me to slow down, absorb my surroundings, and become present and attentive to the sights, sounds, and smells of the world in which I am privileged to live.

Encounters with turtles can be peaceful, sometimes even stultifying, events. They can also be dramatic, like the time I canoed past a big snapping turtle, who, when I touched the nape of its neck with my paddle, shot its head inside its shell, thrashed the water with its legs, churned down into the muck on the lake bottom, and ended up looking like a half-buried, rough-edged rock as the silt slowly settled on top of it.

Probably almost all children know what a turtle is. They learn about these strange animals from seeing pictures of them, reading about turtles in books, and watching nature programs on television. Some children—fewer, alas, each year—are lucky enough to encounter turtles in forests, fields, streams, or ponds. (When I was a boy, I kept box turtles and wood turtles as pets. That's something I wouldn't advise doing today, because even temporarily removing turtles from the wild can harm the turtles, disrupt their reproduction, and endanger local populations.) As we grow older, we become increasingly familiar with the idea of turtles, and we tend to develop certain notions about them: Turtles are stoical, patient, persistent—like the one that bested the impulsive hare in the fabled foot race. Turtles are benign; and while they are indeed benign toward humans, they are less so to an earthworm, crayfish, or slug that's about to become a meal. Turtles have long been the subject of myths and tales. The Ojibway Indians told a story about how the earth was first formed from dirt collected on a turtle's back. For many cultures around the world, turtles have embodied strength, stability, and wisdom. Native peoples have depicted turtles in petroglyphs, pictographs, and designs on fabrics, clay pots, and other objects. They have used turtle shells as containers, rattles, and decorations. Turtles have been eaten as food. (Some still are, in North America and especially in other parts of the world, and a number of species have become endangered as a result.) As adults, many of us stop thinking about turtles. We pretty much take them for granted. In our fast-paced and increasingly mechanized way of life, we rarely encounter them. Yet turtles are fascinating and important creatures, well worth our study and our thoughts—animals about which we need to know more, so that we can keep the world a healthy place for them as well as for many other life forms. We would be much the poorer if turtles did not continue to live among us.

This Wild Guide goes beyond the cursory knowledge and anthropomorphic notions that many people hold about turtles. It explains the physical adaptations that allow a creature to live inside a hard protective shell. It explores the astonishing range of habitats occupied by different species of turtles in North America, including rivers, streams, ponds, estuaries, swamps, bogs, fields, forests, and deserts. It examines feeding, reproduction, and hibernation in turtles. It charts activities throughout the year in various habitats and locales. It gives tips on how to observe turtles, and it suggests ways in which people can help turtles survive in the twenty-first century and beyond. The book also provides a listing of printed and web-based resources concerning turtles.

A species accounts section is included in the center of the book. (See the blue-edged pages.) This mini–field guide describes twenty-two of the more common and distinctive species found on our continent.

Turtle Terms

Taxonomists place turtles in the order Testudines, which falls under Class Reptilia, the reptiles. Reptiles are said to be "cold-blooded," which means they must obtain heat from outside sources, such as the sun or warm water, and must regulate their body temperatures by moving into warmer or cooler settings as needed. Other reptiles include crocodilians (crocodiles and alligators), lizards, and snakes. Turtles are judged to be the oldest and most primitive of the living reptiles. Scientists recognize from 280 to 300 species of turtles existing on earth today—many fewer than the snakes (nearly 3,000 species) and lizards (more than 4,500 species). Currently, turtles are grouped into twelve families; representatives of five of those families can be found in temperate and subtropical North America. (The sea turtles comprise two additional families in Order Testudines. While this book does not focus on sea

TURTLE EVOLUTION

There have been turtles on earth, living inside their shells, for at least 220 million years—long before the dinosaurs' reign ended and before birds and mammals began to evolve. During those ages, continents separated and floated around the globe; inland oceans formed and dried up; mountains rose and fell. Turtles are, quite literally, older than the hills.

As a group turtles have left behind a lot of fossils—largely because a turtle has a large mass of bone that can undergo petrifaction. The earliest turtle fossils have been found in deposits from the Triassic Period of the Paleozoic Era, dated to 220 to 225 million years before the present, in what are now Germany and Thailand. Those turtles appeared to look much like modern snapping turtles. Earlier progenitors have not been located, and the origin of turtles remains a puzzle to evolutionary biologists. The fossil record demonstrates that many kinds of turtles did not survive into modern times. Early turtles had teeth, which today's turtles lack. (Scientists are not sure why turtles "abandoned" teeth.) In past ages there were horned turtles, including one whose skull measured almost two feet across, from one horn tip to the other. The remains of giant land tortoises have been found in Venezuela: creatures with shells measuring 8 feet from end to end. And the fossils of certain extinct sea turtles imply huge swimmers up to 15 feet in length.

Turtles' relatively unspecialized skulls suggest they are close to the ancestral reptilian lineage, and scientists consider them the most primitive reptiles alive today—older and less highly evolved than snakes, lizards, and crocodiles. Today, turtles live on islands scattered throughout the world's oceans, and in Africa, Asia, Europe, South America, North America, and Australia—every continent except Antarctica.

turtles, several species can be spotted along the coasts of our continent, and some individuals nest on North American beaches.)

Carl H. Ernst, Roger W. Barbour, and Jeffrey E. Lovich, coauthors of the definitive reference book *Turtles of the United States and Canada,* identify fifty turtle species as native to North America. Turtles occur in forty-nine of the U.S. states (Alaska does not have turtles); in all of the lower Canadian provinces; and in Mexico. One region particularly rich in turtles lies east of the Mississippi River in Florida and the Gulf Coast states, where around thirty-five species can be found in different habitats—a richness of turtles equaled by only one other part of the world, Southeast Asia.

The word turtle is a general term used to describe all the members of Order Testudines. Another word one hears attached to some turtles is terrapin; this usually refers to small hardshelled turtles, living in aquatic habitats, that people have traditionally collected for food. And when people say tortoise, they are generally talking about land-dwelling turtles, particularly members of the larger species.

1

Reptiles of Distinction

Turtles are unique among vertebrates in having a shell that sheathes and protects their vital parts. A great many aspects of a turtle's body—features both internal and external—have evolved in the service of one key concept: how to accommodate a living, breathing animal inside a more-or-less-rigid protective covering.

Parts of the Shell

A turtle's shell has two main parts. The carapace shields the upper portion of the body, while the plastron protects the lower surfaces. Many turtles have a third section to their shells, the bridge, a bony brace that ties the carapace and plastron together, creating an arch that promotes strength and rigidity in the overall structure.

The carapaces of different kinds of turtles vary greatly. Shapes, when seen from above, range from nearly circular, to oblong, to pear-shaped, to something approaching a rectangle. The box turtle has a high, domed carapace that resembles a soldier's helmet; the softshells possess a flattened carapace that looks like a pancake draped over its occupant. The carapace of the common snapping turtle sports a highly sculpted, triple-keeled surface, while that of the common musk turtle has no bumps or ridges at all. Carapaces display a range of markings and colors, from the murky, nondescript shell of the mud turtle to the boldly patterned one of the river cooter. The plastrons of various kinds of turtles also exhibit different colors and shapes and deliver differing amounts of coverage and protection to the ventral area. In some species, the male's plastron is slightly concave: This shape facilitates mating by letting the male fit more securely atop the female's arched carapace.

Scutes

The word scute sounds odd when attached to a creature that tends to plod along through its environment. But a scute (from the Latin *scutum,* or shield) is actually one of a number of plates covering the outside of a turtle's shell. Most turtles have fifty-four scutes, thirty-eight cloaking the carapace and sixteen covering the plastron. Scutes arise from the epidermis, the outermost layer of skin. They are not bone. Rather, they are composed of the durable protein keratin, the same material that makes up the ever-growing claws and fur of mammals (including the fingernails and hair of humans), the feathers of birds, and the hooves and horns of grazers from cattle to mountain goats.

On my desk lies the shell of a wood turtle found in a thicket along a Pennsylvania stream. The pattern in which its scutes are arranged is typical for most North American turtles. The scutes rimming the edge of the carapace are called marginals—there are twelve opposing pairs of these scutes. A narrow cervical scute stands above the area where the turtle's neck projects. Directly behind the cervical, a row of five vertebrals runs from front to rear, aligned over the center of the turtle's back. Between the vertebrals and the marginals on each side lies a row of four large pleurals. Together, they add up to thirty-eight scutes. (The sixteen scutes of the plastron also have their own names.)

Taxonomists scrutinize the shapes and the layout of turtles' scutes, as well as other physical characteristics, when establishing relationships between different turtle species. For instance, the mud and musk turtles, which make up Family Kinosternidae, have a slightly different arrangement of their scutes compared with other turtles: Instead of a pair of gular scutes at the front of the plastron, these turtles have only a single gular scute. The alligator snapping turtle, an immense and primitive-looking denizen of the Deep South, possesses an extra row of scutes, between the pleurals and marginals of the carapace, which are known as supramarginals. But scutes are not always fail-safe identifiers: The number of scutes may vary occasionally even among members of the same species.

Reptiles are well-known for having scales, and a turtle's scutes can be thought of as extra-large scales. They mesh together like pavers laid edge-to-edge in a tile floor. As a turtle increases in size, each scute also becomes larger. This enlargement takes place when a new layer of keratin forms beneath that of the preceding year, with the new layer's outer edge projecting slightly beyond that of its predecessor. As the years pass, the accumulation of the scutes yields a series of overlapping rings. Each ring is called an annulus (plural, annuli). The annuli appear as concentric polygons arranged around a central nucleus known as the areola. They accrete in much the same way that growth rings build up in tree trunks and in the teeth of some animals. The total number of annuli can indicate the age of a turtle, although it may not be possible to exactly correlate the number of rings with a turtle's years. (The correlation can vary from species to species, between individuals of the same species, from youth to old age, and between individuals living in different habitats or regions.) Some turtles shed the oldest, outermost layer of their

Thirty-eight scutes cover the carapace, or upper shell, of most turtles, including this example of a red-eared slider. The scutes are composed of the durable protein called keratin.

scutes every so often. In general, broad annular rings signify years of rapid growth, while narrow ones indicate slower growth, perhaps made when food was scarce or during periods of ill health. In very old turtles, the most recent annuli can be extremely narrow, and sometimes the rings are worn so smooth that they become almost indistinguishable.

Color pigments deposited in each scute form rays, lines, splashes, bands, or spots, depending on the species of turtle and on the individual animal. Each scute develops its own distinctive pattern, often quite complicated and beautiful. The painted turtles are so named because of the zones of red, yellow, and black coloration in their shells. The turtles known as sliders and cooters display vivid colors and complex designs on their carapaces. Even species that are cloaked in earthen tones, such as the wood turtle and musk turtle, have fascinating patterns in their scutes, discernible if you look closely enough. In most species, both sexes have similar markings and colors. Naturalists use the colors and patterns in turtles' shells to help in identifying the different species.

The Bones Beneath

In addition to my wood turtle paperweight, I have another shell on my desk. This one comes from a box turtle; I found it in the woods when my eye fell upon an ivory-colored object lying on the ground half-covered with dried leaves. After its owner had died, the shell's outer scutes had peeled and fallen off, revealing the bony framework beneath. As C. Kenneth Dodd Jr. explains in his book *North American Box Turtles:* "Unlike in many turtles, the bones of box turtles fuse together, especially in older and larger specimens. Thus, box turtle shells are found in natural settings long after the shells of other turtles would have disarticulated and scattered."

Most turtles have fifty-nine bones in the shell—fifty in the carapace, and another nine in the plastron. (The plastron has four sets of paired bones and one central, roughly circular bone called the entoplastron.) The individual bones abut one another in much the same manner that the scutes do. The bones of the shell, however, are not arranged in an identical pattern to those of the scutes: Instead, the two layers are slightly offset, an arrangement that strengthens the shell in much the same way that the opposed, overlapping layers in a sheet of plywood deliver rigidity and strength.

The bones in a turtle's shell are of two types. One type, dermal bone, develops from an inner layer of skin known as the dermis. The other type, endochondral bone, forms within areas of cartilage. (In humans, dermal bone is found in the face, while the bones of our spinal column, hip and shoulder girdles, and arms and legs are endochondral bone.)

Because my box turtle shell is missing its plastron, when I turn it over I find myself looking at the rounded, vaultlike inner surface of the carapace. Embedded in and fused with the carapace's dermis-derived plates are the endochondral bone of the ribs and vertebral column. The rudimentary ribs look like bony flanges; they merge with and disappear into the plates only

This cutaway view of the shell of a false map turtle shows how the scutes (right) over-lay the bones of the shell (left). The two layers are offset slightly, an arrangement that lends rigidity and strength to the carapace.

about half an inch out from the spinal column. The vertebrae are much more prominent, extending farther downward from the carapace. The vertebrae and ribs somewhat resemble the ridgepole and roof rafters of a house, and, like those framing members, they lend support to the overall structure. It's an odd and a thought-provoking design: ribs and backbone that do not lie between the shoulder and hip girdles, as they do in other vertebrates, but instead have shifted above and outside them. The German turtle scientist Fritz Jürgen Obst puts it this way: "From the internal skeleton of the normal invertebrates, an external skeleton has developed."

As a turtle embryo grows inside the egg, the scutes form before the bony plates do. The ribs extend outward from the nascent vertebral column, piercing the dermis. The bony plates then grow around the rim of the carapace, and ultimately bone tissue fills in to form the arching shell. Some scientists believe that the lower shell, or plastron, includes remnants of the abdominal ribs and the clavicle (the clavicle corresponds to the collarbone in humans). Not all turtles follow this plan exactly. Writes Obst, "It is very often possible to observe in the carapace of individuals surprisingly wide variations from the normal skeletal structure characteristic of the species. 'Surplus' bony plates occur relatively frequently."

Why a Shell?

Florida University ecology professor Nat Frazer notes that many people—including some of the upper-level college biology students that he teaches—are surprised to learn that turtles cannot "leave their shells at will to roam around at faster speeds," as they do in cartoons.

Turtles are completely wedded to their shells, which perform several functions. The most obvious advantage to having a hard shell is being able to hunker down inside it when danger threatens. If a raccoon or a fox comes nosing around, a turtle can quickly withdraw its head and limbs inside its shell and wait until the hunter loses interest and moves on. It requires a huge amount of force, and very strong teeth and jaws, for a predator to crush the arched shell of most of the medium-sized and large adult turtles. Some animals, such as alligators, bears, and feral hogs, can manage the task; most others cannot.

Land-dwelling turtles risk being trod on by larger, heavier animals, and a shell can protect against damage. A high, domed shell—like the one carried by the box turtles—is less apt to be crushed than a lower, flatter shell of the type possessed by many aquatic turtles. The ornate box turtle lives in the Great Plains states from Indiana westward. It often feeds by digging into piles of dung to get at beetles and other insects and their eggs and larvae. Nowadays, ornate box turtles home in on droppings left by cattle—as they presumably exploited the dung of bison and other herd animals over past millennia. The hooves of grazing animals tend to slip off the ornate box turtle's elevated, arching shell. In addition, a prominently domed carapace decreases the ratio of surface area to volume, which limits the amount of moisture that a turtle loses to the environment. For that reason, strongly terrestrial species like the box turtles and the gopher and desert tortoises of the Southeast and Southwest, respectively, have relatively high and rounded shells.

Shells are not fail-safe features providing blanket protection: If a turtle falls from a high ledge, its bones and internal organs can still suffer serious harm, and its shell can sustain damage. A hard shell offers little protection against the tires of cars and trucks (hazards that turtles obviously didn't have to contend with during their evolution). Should a ground fire sweep through grasslands or woods, the shell can minimize damage to a turtle's fleshy parts. (Some turtles bear scars and melted zones on their shells after having survived wildfires. Other turtles perish in fires that are too hot or long-lasting.) Since a shell covers up most of a turtle's skin, it helps the animal avoid becoming dehydrated in sunny or windy habitats and climates.

In winter, many turtles hibernate by burying themselves in mud or sand at the bottoms of ponds and other water bodies. The metabolism of a hibernating turtle slows down radically. For months the creature does not breathe in air (although it draws in some oxygen by other means; the physiology of hibernation will be discussed more fully in chapter 3, "Lifestyles"). The resulting dearth of oxygen results in a buildup of lactic acid. Scientists have discovered that turtles of at least some species draw on minerals in the bones of the shell—compounds that help neutralize the lactic acid, preventing it from damaging body tissues. Some turtles are even able to incorporate the lactic acid into the shell itself. Being able to conserve their oxygen makes it unnecessary for the turtles to interrupt their hibernation and seek out open water where they can surface to breathe in air.

The rounded, flattened shells of aquatic turtles offer little resistance to water, letting them swim proficiently and maneuver while underwater. Some turtles, including several kinds of map turtles, have shells outfitted with sharp spikes and scalloped margins. Probably those features make their owners less palatable to predators. The spikes and knobs may also provide camouflage against a background of aquatic debris or leaf litter. Many turtles have cryptically colored shells with textured surfaces, making them hard to see in specific settings and under certain light conditions. Blending in with its surroundings lets a turtle hide from its enemies and approach its own prey more closely.

So that they can fit inside the confines of an egg, embryonic turtles have shells that are soft and flexible. After hatching, the softness of their shells make young turtles vulnerable to birds' beaks and mammals' jaws. As a turtle grows and matures, its shell gradually hardens. The zones where the bones of the shell meet—areas known as sutures—become more rigid as the zigzag edges of the adjacent bones interlock and meld together.

The resulting shell can be extremely hard, but it may not be completely inflexible. The Central American wood turtle, found from Mexico to Costa Rica, may need to flex its shell in order to lay its extremely large eggs. In North America, the common snapping turtle retains a degree of flexibility in the joints of its smallish, cross-shaped plastron. That flexibility makes it easier for a snapper to fold up its long neck and retract its huge head inside its shell. Unlike many other turtles, however, an adult snapper cannot draw its head fully beneath the sheltering carapace; nor can it retract its tail and limbs completely. Perhaps those reasons explain why snappers are so aggressive and defend themselves so vigorously when threatened.

The softshell turtles of Family Trionychidae do not have a shell, per se. Instead, they have evolved a thick, leathery, highly flexible skin to cover their vitals. Softshells spend most of their lives in the water, often remaining submerged for long periods. At such times, they exchange gases through their leathery skin. One experiment showed that, when underwater, spiny softshells obtained 38 percent of their oxygen and gave off 85 percent of their waste carbon dioxide directly through the skin.

Adding a Hinge

The normal hard shell of a turtle affords its wearer considerable protection. But some species have taken matters a step further by evolving mechanisms for closing the shell entirely. The box turtles of the large and widespread Family Emydidae have a plastron that is divided into two lobes, one in front of the other. Linking the lobes is a movable transverse hinge made of connective tissue. Powerful muscles draw up both the front and back lobes, clapping them against the edge of the carapace and sealing the turtle inside. In their field guide, *Reptiles and Amphibians of Eastern and Central North America*, Roger Conant and Joseph T. Collins observe that box turtles' movable lobes "fit so neatly against the upper shell that in many individuals not even a knife blade [can] be inserted between them."

Musk and mud turtles also belong to Family Kinosternidae. The musk turtles have a plastron with a hinge and two lobes, much like the box turtles. The mud turtles possess a pair of hinges, one behind and the other in front of a fixed lobe running from side to side across the middle of the shell. (The immovable, middle portion of the plastron forms a bridge with the carapace, making the shell more rigid.) The front lobe of the plastron does not shut completely, like that of the box turtle; it does, however, grant a mud turtle greater freedom of movement than it would have if it did not possess a hinged plastron. Blanding's turtle has a hinge across the plastron allowing a pair of lobes to be closed partway—again, not nearly so completely or securely as a box turtle can shut its shell.

Worldwide, turtles in five separate taxonomic families have developed hinges to move parts of their shells up and down, helping them protect their fleshy parts, lay large eggs, or keep their skin from losing moisture rapidly. Turtles that have hinges generally do not possess them when they emerge from the egg as juveniles. Writes Ronald Orenstein in *Turtles, Tortoises, and Terrapins: Survivors in Armor*: "Before a hinge can develop, the scutes and underlying bones must line up in the same spot. In hinged tortoises, the scutes and the bones along the hinge lines do not finish lining up until later in their development, and some individuals never develop a hinge at all." Like scutes and the bony internal plates of the shell, hinges seem to be a rather plastic feature of the morphology of different turtle species. Notes Orenstein: "Hinges have evolved over and over again, even within a single family."

Other External Features

The limbs, tail, neck, and head of most turtles are clad with horny scales similar to those of other reptiles. The scales help cut down on the evaporation of water through the skin. The skin, thick and tough, also retards water loss, particularly in the land-dwelling species. Some aquatic and semiaquatic turtles are adorned with barbels, small projections of skin that hang down below their chins. Mud and musk turtles have these features, as do snapping turtles; scientists are not certain exactly how barbels function, but they suspect the appendages have a sensory function. The alligator snapping turtle possesses a short, forked, pinkish extension on the surface of its tongue. An alligator snapper will lie concealed in the muck on the bottom of a stream or pond with its mouth open; it will twitch and wiggle the tongue extension, which looks like a worm or some other small animal. The appendage lures in small fish, which the turtle captures by suddenly closing its jaws.

Turtles' legs are thick and strong. Most turtles have five toes on each foot. (There are exceptions to this rule: Two subspecies of box turtle have fewer toes: four and three. And the soft-shelled turtles have three toes.) Each toe is tipped with a claw. Claws vary in thickness, length, and shape, according to their primary function. Turtles use their claws to pin down food items, such as carrion, while working with their jaws to tear away flesh. Claws also give purchase when a turtle climbs on a slippery surface, such as a streamside rock or log. In some species, the males have markedly longer claws than the females do; the males vibrate their specialized claws during courtship rituals. Males also use their claws to grip the females' carapaces when mating. Male musk turtles have rough, warty areas on the inner surfaces of their hind legs; these nonslip pads help the male hold onto the edge of the female's shell more securely during mating.

Leg and foot shapes vary considerably between different kinds of turtles. Species that live in rivers and lakes have paddlelike limbs with webbing between the toes, particularly on the hind legs, which provide the main force for propulsion. (This contrasts with the sea turtles, who propel themselves by using their front limbs as flippers.) Gopher and desert tortoises have long, columnar legs, which some observers have likened to the legs of elephants. The short, broad feet of these land dwellers possess heavy claws, and the toes are not webbed. These muscular limbs are built for walking, and they capably transport their owners over rough or sandy terrain. The strong, flattened forelimbs also see duty as shovels, allowing the tortoises to dig burrows, important hideaways in arid habitats and in environments having extremes of heat and cold. Turtles are perhaps unfairly judged to be slow and plodding. It's true that a turtle's shell is relatively heavy and its presence somewhat restricts the mobility of the creature's limbs; but many turtles are surprisingly nimble and can move quickly if the need arises. In some situations, turtles can be downright fast: A softshell or a snapper can strike at prey (or a carelessly placed hand) with astonishing rapidity.

If their overall traveling speed is modest, turtles nevertheless show great endurance, with many land-dwelling species covering hundreds of yards each day. A few freshwater turtles can walk about on land with almost as much felicity as the land-dwelling types. Many aquatic species are also able to climb trees, a useful skill in areas where streamside basking sites are limited. (Basking is an important turtle behavior explained more fully in chapter 3, "Lifestyles.")

The tails of turtles vary in length and thickness. Individuals of some species use their long tails as braces when climbing on rocks and logs. Generally a male turtle of a given species will have a much longer and thicker tail than a female of the same species. On the underside of the tail, between the shell's outer rim and the tail's tip, lies the cloaca, the shared opening for both the reproductive and digestive tracts in reptiles. The male's penis is housed in the cloacal cavity, and the tail must be large enough to contain this structure. A male with a long tail can more easily work himself into a position to bring his penis into contact with the female's cloaca. A male may attach himself to a female by wrapping his tail around hers. The tails of some turtles have a hard, pointed tip, known as a nail; during mating, the male yellow musk turtle gains stability by inserting his sharp-tipped tail under the edge of the female's carapace.

Turtles' necks are muscular and highly flexible. Some species have relatively long necks, such as the diamondback terrapin, the softshells, and the snapping turtles, while others have shorter necks. No matter how long or short their necks may be, all turtles possess eight neck vertebrae. The North American species (as well as most other turtles worldwide) are considered to be cryptodires, or "hidden-necks." When retracting the head and neck into the shell, the neck of a cryptodire bends into a vertical S-curve, so that the neck withdraws completely out of sight. Another group of turtles, found in South America, Africa, Madagascar, and Australia, bend their necks around to the side, tucking their heads sideways beneath the rim of the shell. These turtles are known as pleurodires, or "side-necks."

Turtles have muscles attached to their skulls for opening and shutting their eyelids; moving and focusing their eyes; and opening and closing their jaws. Like other reptiles and birds, turtles can be said to be poker-faced: They lack the complex arrays of facial muscles and soft tissues that mammals use to fine-tune the movements and positioning of eyes, muzzles, snouts, lips, and ears that are so important in conveying emotions and intentions. Since turtles are less social than mammals, they do not need to send complex facial signals.

Fossils reveal that during the Triassic Period (between 230 and 195 million years before the present), at least some types of prototurtles possessed teeth—although the teeth were rudimentary, apparently already having dwindled by that point in their evolution. Today, no turtles retain teeth. Instead, their jaws are sheathed with the tough protein keratin. Depending on how they are

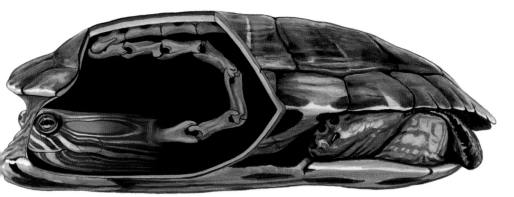

When a turtle pulls its head back inside its protective shell, its muscular, highly flexible neck bends into a vertical S-curve.

used, a turtle's jaws may have sharp edges (for shearing flesh or plant matter), they may be broad and flattened (for crushing hard animal items such as mollusks), or they may have serrated surfaces (to grind up plant parts efficiently). Turtles' jaws attach to robust muscles anchored to the skull. In most turtles, the skull curves outward at the temporal region, providing a space behind and slightly below the eye socket to house the jaw muscles. These spaces, one on each side of the skull, are called embayments.

Turtles' jaws do not show as much variation in shape as do birds' beaks, but their shapes often hint at their uses. In snapping turtles, the upper jawbone curves downward to form a prominent hook for latching onto prey, including, at times, animals as large and strong as muskrats and waterfowl. This "grabhook" functions much like the sharply hooked beaks of eagles, hawks, and vultures. In softshell turtles, fleshy upper lips cover and protect the extremely sharp-edged jaws, which are used for cutting up the flesh of fish, frogs, and crayfish, and for processing certain plant foods.

Some turtles have prominent snouts. The softshells bury themselves in mud or sand at the bottoms of streams; thus hidden, they extend their necks upward so that their long, tubular snouts just reach the surface to snorkel in air. A softshell so situated can wait indefinitely for prey to happen past. Softshells—as well as several other North American species, including the chicken turtle—also use their long, voluminous necks as underwater vacuum cleaners to suck in small aquatic animals as prey.

Senses and Intelligence

As far as we can tell, turtles have keen senses. They detect light readily, adjusting their behaviors to different light levels. Their vision is acute, particularly at short ranges, and many species can perceive movement at surprisingly long distances. Turtles see well both underwater and in the open air. Experiments indicate that at least some species possess color vision, often with a heightened ability to detect colors toward the red end of the spectrum and even into the infrared range. The ability to discern colors probably helps turtles during social interactions, including finding mates of the same species: Consider the fact that many turtles have bright markings on the shell, head, and limbs. Color vision also helps turtles find food. In some species, it may even let them discriminate between ripe and unripe fruits.

Spatial discrimination seems to vary between species. Early studies found that box turtles hesitated at the edge of a precipice, whereas painted turtles plunged right over. These actions can be explained by behavioral patterns and habitat preferences: Painted turtles often launch themselves off basking perches into the water, while highly terrestrial box turtles need to travel safely across broken, often hilly terrain.

In turtles, the areas of the brain that are associated with the sense of smell are significantly larger than the same areas in other reptiles. Most biologists believe that turtles have at least an adequate, and probably an excellent, sense of smell. Water is a good medium for carrying and dispersing dissolved odorous compounds. Smaller turtles use their olfactory sense to detect larger aquatic turtles, such as the predatory alligator snapper, and discreetly swim or walk away. Underwater, turtles can find food in the dark by homing in on odors; land turtles are also able to detect food by smell. Turtles employ their sense of smell to recognize members of the same species and to locate potential mates. Turtles possess a Jacobson's organ, or vomeronasal organ. (Amphibians, other reptiles, and some mammals also have a Jacobson's organ.) This specialized structure includes a region of sensitive nerve endings that can detect minute quantities of chemical particles; in turtles, it is housed in the same chamber as the nasal membranes.

External ears are not visible on turtles, and at one time people thought turtles were quite deaf. Some species show a large, circular area on each side of the head behind the eyes: This tympanic membrane covers the middle and inner ears. Most turtles—probably all of them—can hear to at least some extent. Not infrequently I have come upon a box turtle with its head and legs retracted and its shell half closed, apparently waiting for me to approach; while trying to sneak up on basking aquatic turtles, I've heard them splash into the water well before I arrived. Maybe those turtles actually heard me. Or perhaps their inner ears detected low-frequency vibrations caused by my footfalls. But obviously some vibration-activated sense had alerted them to my presence. Turtles do not possess vocal cords, but they can and do make sounds. In some cases the sounds seem to be involuntary, as when a turtle quickly pulls its head and limbs inside its shell, pushing the air out of its lungs with an audible hiss. Observers have also reported turtles producing various whistles, grunts, and whines, but biologists do not know whether these vocalizations play a role in communicating.

It's clear that turtles do have a keen sense of heat and cold—a faculty of critical importance to a cold-blooded, or ectothermic, creature that must regulate its body temperature by frequently moving from hot to cool microhabitats and vice versa. An acute temperature sense is also needed by an animal that must locate nesting sites that are suitably warm for the development of its eggs.

Are turtles intelligent? This question has long been debated. Certainly their directional senses and homing and navigational abilities are superb. Individuals of some species have learned to move through mazes as quickly as laboratory rats—although this behavior may indicate an advanced spatial sense as much as an ability to solve problems. Pet turtles adapt easily to being fed, and some find ways to alert their keepers when they are hungry. In general, behavioral scientists judge turtles as having a level of intelligence typical for the reptiles.

Breathing

Most vertebrates have a flexible rib cage that allows the lungs to expand and contract during breathing. Not so the turtles, who long ago traded away flexible ribs in favor of a fixed, protective shell. Various species of turtles have evolved different means of drawing air into their lungs. Turtles have also developed indirect ways of obtaining oxygen during times when they are sealed away from contact with the air, as when hibernating or remaining underwater.

In turtles, the lungs lie just beneath the carapace and above the other internal organs. The upper surface of the lungs attaches to the carapace itself, while the lower portion is joined to the viscera (heart, liver, stomach, and intestinal tract) by a skin of connective tissue known as the diaphragmaticus. The viscera themselves are also contained within a membrane that attaches to the diaphragmaticus. Groups of muscles rhythmically change the volume of the abdominal cavity. One set of muscles moves the viscera upward, pushing air out of the lungs. Then other muscles contract, pulling the viscera away from the lungs, which lets the lungs expand and draw in air.

When turtles walk about, the motions of their forelimbs promote the suction-and-compression actions that ventilate the lungs. A turtle can change its lung volume simply by drawing its limbs inward, then extending them outward again: Turtles floating on top of the water often can be seen moving their legs in and out, which helps them breathe. A turtle pulled back inside its shell has no room in its lungs for air. At these and other times, turtles use different strategies to obtain oxygen.

One aid to respiration is the hyoid apparatus, a system of bony and cartilaginous rods located at the base of the tongue. Raising and lowering the hyoid apparatus causes a turtle's throat to rise and fall, pulling in air. (In addition to promoting ventilation, this air movement allows a turtle to better use its sense of smell.) In the highly aquatic softshell turtles, the throat is lined with fingerlike projections of skin called villi, which are richly supplied with blood. The villi work like gills, expelling carbon dioxide and taking in oxygen from the water. To process oxygen-rich water, a softshell uses its hyoid apparatus to repeatedly fill and empty its throat in a process known as buccopharyngeal breathing. When underwater, a softshell typically pumps water in and out about sixteen times per minute. Turtles that hibernate underwater also exchange gases through the throat lining, cycling the water inside the throat cavity several times each minute. Many turtles practice buccopharyngeal breathing, and some turtles even take in oxygen through the cloaca.

Many of the details of turtles' breathing remain unknown. What is clear, however, is that different kinds of turtles have evolved different methods of fulfilling their oxygen needs. Through evolution, they have gotten very good at obtaining this essential gas. As Ronald Orenstein notes in *Turtles, Tortoises, and Terrapins: Survivors in Armor,* turtles seem able to breathe "with the least amount of effort no matter what their circumstances."

Size

North American turtles vary widely in size. Among the smallest are the musk turtles, a group found mainly in the eastern half of the continent. In the common musk turtle, adults are only 2 to $4^1/2$ inches long. Smaller yet is the bog turtle, with a carapace scarcely longer than 3 inches. At the other end of the scale is the alligator snapping turtle. This southern species often reaches 2 feet long, with a record length of $31^1/2$ inches. The heaviest wild alligator snapper on record weighed a whopping 316 pounds. The alligator snapper is one of the largest freshwater turtles in the world.

Reptiles grow throughout their lives, although growth rates slow tremendously in very old individuals. In most turtle species, the females are larger than the males—an example of a common animal trait called sexual dimorphism. In some groups, such as the painted turtles and map turtles, the females are markedly larger—up to one and a half times and in some cases even twice the size of the males. In other groups, including land tortoises and mud turtles, there is often very little difference in size between the sexes. In the snapping turtles, both sexes have the potential to achieve the same very large body size. And in a few species, such as the bog turtle and wood turtle, males tend to be slightly larger than same-age females.

Longevity

Hatchling turtles are preyed on by a host of animals, and few survive to reach adult size. But once they attain maturity, turtles have the physiological potential to live for a long time. Biologists have estimated that more than 80 percent of adults in some species typically will survive from one year to the next. In the smaller turtles, the normal lifespan is probably around thirty to forty years. Box turtles have been documented to have survived for over a century. Snapping turtles may live for half a century and perhaps much longer. In captivity, Blanding's turtles have lived seventy-seven years and musk turtles have survived fifty-four years. Few studies have been done to accurately determine the longevity of different species of turtles in the wild. One thing is clear, however: Turtles live much longer than do birds and mammals of a similar size.

2
Habitats

In the book *Turtle Conservation,* in a chapter entitled "Primary and Secondary Effects of Habitat Alteration," biologists Joseph C. Mitchell and Michael W. Klemens define habitat as "the physical and biological environment used by a population of turtles." For example, a part of the Mojave Desert in southern California wherein dwells a population of desert tortoises constitutes only one type of habitat used by this species across its geographic range. An ecosystem, such as the Northern Hardwood Forest or the Florida Everglades, "usually encompasses more habitat types than are used by a population of turtles," write Mitchell and Klemens. "Thus, a habitat is a component of an ecosystem."

As a group, turtles show an impressive ability to occupy a variety of habitats in most of the ecosystems of North America. Streams and rivers, swamps and bogs, prairies, thickets, humid forests, treeless deserts—one or more species of turtle can be found in all of those settings. The only region that turtles have not exploited is the far North, where no reptiles or amphibians exist, because at certain times of the year temperatures become too frigid for "cold-blooded," or ectothermic, animals to survive. For the same reason, turtles are not found at high elevations in the mountains.

In the Water

Most North American turtles spend much of their lives in freshwater: ponds, lakes, springs, streams, creeks, rivers, oxbows, fens, bogs, swamps, ditches, canals, sloughs, bays. A few species venture into deep water and swift currents, but most stick to the shallows and areas where the current isn't too strong. The largest family of turtles on our continent (and in the world) is

Different species of turtles occupy different habitats, including the land, shallow water, and deeper water.

Emydidae, also known as the pond, marsh, semiaquatic, or water turtles, standing or moving water being a necessary component of their existence. The United States has seven genera and twenty-six species of semiaquatic turtles. This diverse tribe includes cooters, sliders, diamondback terrapins, and Blanding's, chicken, painted, redbelly, map, spotted, and bog turtles. While all of these turtles can be strongly aquatic, they also use the land at times. These species are amphibious, needing water for certain aspects of their life cycles, such as feeding and mating, and requiring dry land for other behaviors, including basking (regulating the body temperature through exposure to the sun's warmth) and nesting and laying eggs. (Two other more-terrestrial groups in Family Emydidae are the box and wood turtles.)

As a habitat, freshwater is a fairly safe and productive setting. In addition to the Emydidae, most other families of North American turtles also depend on standing or moving water. Snapping turtles (Family Chelydridae) occupy both freshwater and brackish habitats. Most species of musk and mud turtles (Family Kinosternidae) rarely leave the water, except during rainy spells and to lay their eggs on land. Softshell turtles (Family Trionychidae) are even more firmly wedded to the water than are the semiaquatic turtles: About the only times that softshells leave their aquatic realm are to bask on shore—always within a split-second dash of the water—and to dig nests and lay eggs in nearby sand or gravel bars.

Some turtles prefer smaller bodies of water. The bog turtle is a small turtle inhabiting bogs, marshes, and damp grassy fields and meadows with slow-moving streams fed by pure springs, in both lowland and upland settings. In those pocket wetlands, bog turtles rarely need to compete for food or basking sites with larger turtles, which normally use other areas. Bog turtle populations can become quite dense: A study in New Jersey found twenty to twenty-five bog turtles per acre of suitable habitat.

Another turtle that often uses small, shallow water bodies is the spotted turtle. This diminutive turtle—at 3 1/2 to 4 1/2 inches, only about an inch longer than the bog turtle—inhabits pools, ponds, seasonal wetlands, ditches, wet meadows, and slow sections of streams. It often shares those habitats with painted, musk, mud, and snapping turtles. On land near the water, it may be found in proximity to box turtles and wood turtles.

A large body of water—a big pond, a lake, a reservoir, or a high-volume creek or river—may offer many ecological niches supporting a range of species. Competition is reduced by different kinds of turtles preferring specific microhabitats, such as shallow water, deep water, a soft mucky bottom, a sandy bottom, rocky areas, or dense vegetation; by different daily or seasonal activity peaks; and by different feeding techniques or food preferences. In some locales—subtropical Florida, for instance—aquatic habitats may produce food abundantly year-round. In such rich habitats, turtles of similar species may live side by side, feeding on the same plants or animals. Some freshwater turtles spend most of their lives on—and in—the layers of mud and decomposed organic matter that accumulate on the bottoms of slow rivers and beneath the still waters of lakes and ponds. The musk and mud turtles thrive in such dim, murky places. Not particularly adept at swimming, musk and mud turtles stalk along on the bottom, hunting for mollusks, worms, aquatic insects, and other small invertebrates. Musk and mud turtles feed most actively at night. Kept almost perpetually wet, the dark-colored shells of these bottom specialists often support a thick growth of algae, making the turtles extremely hard to spot. Their habitat, nocturnal habits, and cryptic colors render them so unobtrusive that, although they may be plentiful in a given lake or pond, they may be seen by humans only rarely.

The common musk turtle, the most widespread species among the musk and mud turtles, inhabits many waterways in eastern North America and has a range that stretches from southern Canada to Florida and west to Kansas and Texas. The razorback musk turtle lives in rivers, slow streams, and swamps in eastern Texas, Oklahoma, Arkansas, Louisiana, and Mississippi. The loggerhead musk turtle makes its home in similar environs in Florida, Georgia, and Alabama, while the stripeneck musk turtle ranges from western Georgia to Mississippi and north along the border between North Carolina and Tennessee. The flattened musk turtle is a curious specimen, possessing a much flatter shell than those of the other musk turtles. The flattened musk turtle has been found in just one river system, the Black Warrior, in central Alabama, where it thrives in clear, rock-bottomed streams at higher elevations—something of a departure from the murky, muddy haunts of its relatives.

Most North American turtles, such as the western painted turtle, spend their lives in and near fresh water. In general, the water is a fairly safe and productive habitat.

Of the musk and mud turtles, the latter are more apt to prowl about on dry land. The eastern mud turtle lives in the Mid-Atlantic states and the Southeast, where it favors the shallow waters of ditches, sloughs, streams, lagoons, bayous, Carolina bays, and cypress swamps. Mud turtles can tolerate brackish water, and some individuals living along the coast or on barrier islands take up residence in tidal marshes. Mud turtles often rest inside muskrat lodges. Particularly in the spring and fall, they may leave the water to hunt for invertebrate prey on land. In winter, many mud turtles hibernate inside rotten logs, in clumps of dead leaves, and in burrows in the soil, rather than under the water, as most of the semiaquatic turtles do. In summer, if their aquatic habitats dry out, mud turtles may estivate, or become dormant, either by burrowing into mud at the edge of swamp or pond or resorting to the same microhabitats on land where they often spend the winter.

Snapping turtles are at home in just about any freshwater habitat. They prefer a soft, mucky bottom in a fairly shallow zone, where they can shift their bulky bodies back and forth until they become half-buried in the mud. Camouflaged by the mud and by its rough, ridged shell, a snapper will lie in wait for passing prey with only its eyes and snout showing; now and then the turtle will extend its long neck upward, break the surface of the water with its nostrils, and snitch a breath. Snappers take advantage of any cover their habitat offers, lurking beneath submerged tree roots and stumps and among debris and aquatic plants. Snappers are tough and adaptable. They colonize polluted waters where other turtles cannot survive. They also venture into the brackish mouths of tidal rivers and creeks that exchange water with the ocean, and some even swim briefly in the saltwater bays between barrier islands and the mainland.

The diamondback terrapin lives along the Atlantic and Gulf coasts in salt marshes, estuaries, and tidal creeks. A suite of behavioral, physiological, and anatomical adaptations let this species thrive in brackish water. It seems able to discriminate between waters of different salinities: When its own body is charged with salt, it will selectively drink from a source having a low salinity. Blood, intracellular fluids, and muscle tissue work in concert to keep the body's salt content from becoming too high. In winter, diamondback terrapins often hibernate buried in the mud of creek banks near the high tide line. This species commonly nests in vegetated dunes facing away from the sea. After they hatch, juvenile diamondback terrapins hide themselves beneath mats of wrack and flotsam floating in tidal creeks.

Three species of softshell turtles occur in North America. With their flattened carapaces and flexible leathery skin, these turtles can swim and maneuver adroitly in the water. The smooth softshell prefers larger streams and rivers with moderate to fast currents, and lives in the Ohio, Mississippi, and Missouri river drainages of the Midwest. The spiny softshell occupies creeks and rivers in much of central America, and it also lives in the still waters of lakes, bayous, oxbows, and impoundments. The Florida softshell, found in Florida and in parts of Alabama, Georgia, and South Carolina, uses most of the freshwater habitats within its range, including the bubbling mud and sand springs for which the Florida peninsula is famous. In coastal areas, Florida softshells also venture into brackish zones. All of the softshell species prefer a muddy or sandy bottom, where they can bury themselves and lie in wait for prey.

Most water-dwelling turtles require some vegetation in their habitat—plants to eat or plants that attract and nourish prey; plants that provide the turtles with cover in which to conceal themselves, either to ambush prey or to avoid their own predators. Blanding's turtle inhabits lakes, ponds, marshes, and creeks having a soft but firm organic bottom with plenty of vegetation. Blanding's turtle rarely uses ponds with bare sand bottoms and no vegetation. It also avoids wetlands where the vegetation is too thick, such as areas choked with cattails; when muskrats clear away cattails through their feeding, Blanding's turtles may then begin to forage in those areas.

A habitat feature vital for many aquatic and semiaquatic turtles is an adequate supply of basking sites. Turtles need places where they can haul themselves out of the water and lie soaking up the rays of the sun. Turtles bask on rocks, sandbars, sand and gravel beaches and banks, masses of decomposing cattail stems or other aquatic vegetation floating in the water, brush drifted against a bank, fallen tree trunks, and half-submerged branches. Basking areas must be close enough to the water so that turtles can quickly escape from land predators. Some preferred basking sites have been used by generation after generation of turtles. Map turtles depend heavily on basking features—so much so that some species spend their nights floating in the water, anchored to an emergent chunk of wood with their claws. They often bask for much of the day, using dead wood as a perch, including shoreline debris and snags sticking up out of the water some distance from the shore.

In general, the farther north you go in North America, the smaller the number of turtle species you will find using strictly aquatic habitats. In the Northeast, many pond turtles live a partially terrestrial life to take advantage of the warmer summer temperatures on land—warmth that helps speed up body processes and life cycles. Farther south, higher ambient temperatures make life easier for aquatic turtles, with many species spending most of their annual cycle in the water. The part of North America richest in water-dwelling turtles is the Southeast. For eons, this region has had a stable climate, and it has not been subject to mountain-building processes or to the advance and retreat of glaciers, catastrophic events that destroyed many plants and animals farther to the north. (Eastern Asia is another area particularly rich in turtles, for the same reasons that the U.S. Southeast has retained such a wealth of species. Both regions also have a great diversity of other reptiles, amphibians, and plants.)

On the Land

In North America, two types of semiaquatic turtles in Family Emydidae, the wood turtle and the box turtle, have taken up what is essentially a dry-land existence. Not all of these turtles shun watery places, however; some individuals enter the water every few days during the period when they are most active, and many remain near water sources and submerge themselves during hot weather.

The wood turtle occurs in the Upper Midwest and the Northeast, in forested areas through which streams or rivers flow. In Michigan and Wisconsin, wood turtles spend much of their time in the water, where they prefer a hard sand or gravel bottom to a mucky or soft clay substrate. In the eastern part of the species' range, as summer temperatures rise, wood turtles spend increasing amounts of time on land—but even then, they rarely venture far from rivers, streams, swamps, bogs, or wet meadows. Wood turtles use alder thickets, deciduous forests, and coniferous woodlands; they enter hemlock stands when mushrooms, a favorite food, sprout abundantly. When the weather gets really hot, the turtles soak themselves in the water to cool off and to prevent the loss of moisture through the skin. Wood turtles can swim competently and are at home in the water whenever they need to be. A study in Pennsylvania found that wood turtles spent more time in the water than in any single type of land habitat. Some wood turtles hibernate underwater, either resting on the bottom of a stream or pond or buried in mud or sand. Others spend the winter on land, digging into soil beneath overhanging roots and streamside logs, and sleeping inside beaver lodges and muskrat burrows.

The eastern box turtle inhabits open woods, pastures, marshy meadows, and, in Florida, palmetto thickets. Although generally more terrestrial than the wood turtle, the box turtle still likes to have access to water. In summer, box turtles may linger on the edge of a pond (or even in a puddle), soaking themselves when temperatures soar. Box turtles in Florida and along the Gulf Coast are particularly fond of the water. Box turtles do not hesitate to swim across streams and ponds when shifting about within their home ranges. One researcher studying habitat selection by box turtles in Arkansas found that the turtles used grasslands in late spring and early fall, and forested areas in early spring, summer, and late fall. After recording the temperature, vegetative cover, and moisture of different areas frequented by the turtles, the scientist concluded that box turtles remain within a fairly narrow microclimatic range at all times during their annual activity period.

Spotted turtles are generally considered to be pond dwellers, but many of them also spend considerable time on the land. In central Massachusetts, spotted turtles winter in swamps grown up with red maple and sphagnum moss. In the spring, the turtles head for temporary pools, such as basins and low areas that fill with snowmelt and rain, where they feed on the larvae of aquatic insects. Many individuals travel 400 feet overland, or farther, to arrive at those feeding hot spots. The turtles remain in and near the temporary ponds until the ponds start drying up in midsummer, at which time the turtles head back toward the swamps where they will winter. On the way, they may rest on land, in shallow forms among grasses or beneath leaf litter, for several days or even a couple of weeks.

In the northern part of their range, chicken turtles leave their ponds in the summer and travel overland, stopping and burying themselves in mud or

Desert tortoises avoid extremes of heat and cold by sheltering inside their burrows, which these terrestrial turtles dig using their large, strong forelimbs.

moist sand for as long as two weeks. In eastern Tennessee, a female bog turtle fitted with a radio transmitter went walking around for thirty-seven days, moving more than 2½ miles from her home wetlands. She amazed the scientists who were tracking her by climbing up and over two steep mountain ridges and crossing the Appalachian Trail. Sadly, this little traveler was struck by a vehicle and probably killed while crossing a road; only the damaged transmitter was found.

The four members of Family Testudinidae living on our continent—the desert tortoise, bolson tortoise, Texas tortoise, and gopher tortoise—are almost completely terrestrial.

As their name suggests, desert tortoises have evolved to live in that less-than-hospitable environment, the desert. In different parts of the species' range, the tortoises use different habitat features, including valleys, flats, alluvial fans, and rocky slopes and hillsides. Desert tortoises withstand extreme heat and aridity by going underground, digging burrows in which they spend much of their lives. A key aspect of a tortoise habitat is soil of a type in which a tortoise can readily dig; dry, gravelly or sandy soils are best. A tortoise will scrape the soil aside with its forelimbs, and remove soil from the excavation using its front legs or by shoving the material away with the sides of its shell. Desert tortoises often site their burrows beneath bushes, in the banks of arroyos, or at the bases of cliffs. Taller vegetation in tortoise habitats may include creosote bush, cheese bush, saltbush, hop sage, paloverde, ironwood, smoke tree, and cacti; among these shrubs and small trees grow the grasses and annual and perennial plants upon which the tortoises feed.

The bolson tortoise is named for a specific landscape feature: A bolson is a flat, arid valley ringed by mountains and draining into a shallow lake. (The term comes from a Spanish word meaning purse or pouch, describing the characteristic shape of the valley.) The bolson tortoise lives only in the Bolsón de Mapimí, a remote basin in the Chihuauan Desert of northcentral Mexico.

The Texas tortoise lives in semidesert habitats in Mexico and in scrub forests and brushland in southern Texas. While a number of human activities can spell harm for the habitat of the Texas tortoise, the managed grazing of cattle is often helpful, as light overgrazing encourages the growth of prickly pear, a staple summer food.

The gopher tortoise occurs on the southeastern coastal plain from South Carolina to Florida and west to Louisiana. It lives in xeric, or dry, habitats including longleaf pine sandhills, oak hammocks, scrublands, pine flatwoods, prairies, and coastal dunes. Gopher tortoises also use some human-created habitats: pastures, old fields, and grassy roadside areas. Three basic requirements are well-drained, deep, sandy soils, in which the tortoises can dig their burrows; herbaceous food plants; and open, sunny areas for basking and nesting. Periodic natural fires help maintain gopher tortoise habitat by opening up the tree canopy, letting sunlight reach the ground and spurring the growth of forage plants.

Like its close relative the desert tortoise, the gopher tortoise digs a burrow for a shelter. Inside the burrow, temperature and humidity stay fairly constant year-round, insulating its occupant from climate extremes on the surface. Gopher tortoises' burrowing, mound building (a mound often builds up at the mouth of the burrow), and grazing can alter a habitat. A study in oak-and-pine sandhill woodlands in Florida found that areas where tortoises dug their burrows were lower in soil nutrients and organic matter and had markedly greater daily temperature swings than nearby undisturbed areas. Temperatures during prescribed (human-caused-and-monitored) fires were significantly lower on the bare mounds and near the burrow openings than in the more heavily vegetated adjacent areas. Also, a greater diversity of plants grew in the area of the diggings.

Gopher tortoise burrows can be 40 feet long and 10 feet deep, although most are shorter and shallower than that. A tortoise may dig several burrows during its lifetime. The burrows provide living space for a wide range of other animals. More than 360 kinds of creatures have been documented using gopher tortoise burrows, including arthropods (spiders, ticks, and insects); amphibians (frogs and toads); other reptiles (snakes and lizards); birds (burrowing owls and quail); and mammals (opossums, mice, rats, skunks, weasels, and many others). Some species, such as the Florida mouse, seemingly cannot survive in the absence of gopher tortoise burrows. (A wide range of animals also live in the burrows of desert tortoises in the U.S. Southwest.)

Habitat Loss

In North America, there is no greater threat to turtles than the degradation and destruction of the places where they live. Both aquatic and terrestrial species have lost vast amounts of habitat, particularly in the last century, as humans have increased in numbers and have radically changed the landscape.

Large-scale agriculture has destroyed countless acres of land formerly inhabited by turtles and other species of wildlife. In the Rio Grande Valley of Texas, over 90 percent of the semidesert scrub habitat used by the Texas tortoise has been eliminated, mainly through the expansion of farming operations. (Fortunately for the Texas tortoise, habitats remain healthy in areas where cattle grazing predominates.) In Florida, the habitat of the gopher tortoise is being chewed away by farming operations (including creating citrus plantations out of former acres of sandy scrub), urban development, road building, phosphate mining, sand extraction, and military activities. Turtles living in wetlands die out when bogs and swamps are drained to create farm fields or housing developments. Even seasonal or ephemeral wetlands—now under assault from people who claim these areas are not truly wetlands, and want them opened up for development—can be critical places for a wide range of turtle species (as well as many other wild animals) during times of the year when these small, subtle features hold water. Pollution from garbage, sewage, and road runoff can harm or destroy habitats. When streams are channelized or dredged, their flow patterns are changed and their natural complexity is lost, including a diversity of vegetation—plants that turtles eat, plants that are consumed by the creatures turtles prey on. If the damming of rivers floods marshy ground and low-lying thickets and woodlands, shallow-water and wetland, as well as terrestrial, habitats are lost. When humans develop coastal areas, they destroy habitats and the shellfish prey of diamondback terrapins and ruin their nesting areas. Unfortunately for the bog turtle, many acres of its living space have been drained for agriculture, roads, housing, and other development, obliterating many local populations and landing this small reptile on the federal endangered species list (the U.S. Fish and Wildlife Service considers the bog turtle to be "threatened" rangewide) and on the endangered species lists of a number of states.

Alien plants have overspread many wetlands, rendering habitats unfit for turtles and other wildlife species. Purple loosestrife is a European import that has invaded wetlands in eastern North America—particularly ones that have been drained or disturbed. Purple loosestrife quickly crowds out native vegetation, resulting in a dense monoculture that offers little or nothing for turtles; many acres of bog turtle habitat have been destroyed or damaged by this

SEA TURTLES

Six kinds of sea turtles, all of them in Family Cheloniidae, visit the coasts of North America. Sea turtles can be huge—over 6 feet long and weighing 2,000 pounds, in the case of the leatherback. Sea turtles have sleek, streamlined shells. They use their flattened forelimbs like oars to propel themselves through the water, and they maneuver using their rudderlike hind limbs. They are powerful swimmers, and individuals migrate long distances through the open ocean.

Sea turtles eat crabs, clams and other shellfish, jellyfish, and fish. Some species consume seaweed and aquatic grasses. Both young and adults are hunted and eaten by sharks, large fish, and a few marine mammals. Sea turtles mate in the ocean. The females then home in on specific nesting areas on coastal beaches, in some cases navigating hundreds of miles to get there. A gravid female crawls onto the shore, usually as far as the dune front; above the high-tide line she digs a hole using her hind flippers, lays eggs in the hole, scrapes sand over the nest chamber, and returns to the sea. Females usually lay several clutches totaling fifty to two hundred spherical eggs over a period of several weeks. Many predators raid sea turtle nests, including birds, canines, felines, raccoons, and feral pigs. The young hatch after about two months' incubation. Usually the hatchlings emerge at night; attracted by open areas of illumination, the young turtles head toward the ocean. On their way to the water, and after entering it, the juveniles are preyed on heavily by birds, mammals, crabs, and fishes.

Humans' activities are the main cause of sea turtle mortality and the reason why all six of the following species are considered either threatened or endangered worldwide. The list of human-caused hazards is long: fishing and shrimping nets that ensnare and drown turtles, trash and debris that turtles eat or get tangled up in, pollution, oil slicks, beach development that destroys nesting areas, and direct killing for food. I once found a loggerhead that had washed ashore, dead, at Cocoa Beach, Florida; a deep gash in its head showed where a boat propeller had killed it, a not-uncommon accident.

The green turtle *(Chelonia mydas)* is named for the color of its body fat. (The green turtle is an important source of food in many third-world nations where protein is scarce.) Adults are 36 to 60 inches long and weigh 250 to 650 pounds. Although few green turtles stray from the tropics, individuals have shown up along the shores of eastern North America from the Florida Keys to Massachusetts and along the Pacific Coast. A population resides in San Diego Bay, California, from around November to April. More green turtles are seen in northern parts of the Pacific during El Niño years, when ocean temperatures become unusually warm. Green turtles have nested on beaches in Texas, Florida, Georgia, and North Carolina; they nest regularly on many of the Caribbean islands and the coasts of Central and South America.

The hawksbill *(Eretmochelys imbricata)* is named for its long, narrow snout, which resembles a hawk's beak. This turtle can reach 3 feet in length and can weigh up to 280 pounds, although most adults weigh 95 to 165 pounds. In their tropical homes, hawksbill turtles live along rocky coastlines and coral reefs and in estuaries and mud-bottomed lagoons; they feed mainly on the stationary marine animals known as sponges.

(continued on page 26)

(continued from page 25)
Most nesting sites are in the tropics, including the Caribbean, and nests have also been found on Florida beaches. The species ranges as far north as the waters off Massachusetts and California.

The loggerhead *(Caretta caretta)*, named for its large head, is 31 to 45 inches long and weighs 170 to 500 pounds. This turtle ranges as far north as Newfoundland and Alaska. The most abundant sea turtles on the East Coast, loggerheads travel up the Chesapeake Bay from May to November and may enter the mouths of major rivers draining into the Bay. In the Chesapeake, juvenile loggerheads feed mainly on horseshoe crabs; scientists estimate that 2,000 to 10,000 loggerheads use the Bay each year. Along the coast, they swim in the channels between barrier islands, and in lagoons between the islands and the mainland. The loggerhead regularly nests on beaches in the Carolinas and rarely as far north as New Jersey.

Kemp's ridley *(Lepidochelys kempii)*, also known as the Atlantic ridley, is 23 to 29 inches long and weighs 80 to 110 pounds. Kemp's ridleys live in the Gulf of Mexico and in the warm waters of the Gulf Stream off the Atlantic coast. From 300 to 500 immature Kemp's ridleys are believed to migrate into the Chesapeake Bay each summer, where they feed mainly on blue crabs in eelgrass beds. The Chesapeake is a critically important habitat for this species. Most nesting for the entire species takes place at Rancho Nuevo, Tamaulipas, Mexico. Nesting has been reported from Texas, Florida, and South Carolina. The Kemp's ridley is considered to be the most endangered species of marine turtle: In the 1940s, as many as 40,000 females were nesting at Rancho Nuevo; in 1994, the herpetologist Carl Ernst estimated that only 2,000 mature females still survived. Why these turtles are called "ridleys" is not known; "Kemp" is for Richard Kemp, a nineteenth-century Florida naturalist who collected the type, or first, specimen.

The Pacific ridley *(Lepidochelys olivacea)*, also called the olive ridley, grows to a maximum length of about 29 inches. It lives in tropical waters of the Indian and Pacific oceans and gets as far north as Oregon and perhaps farther during El Niño years. In North America, nesting occurs as far north as Baja, Mexico. Pacific ridley populations have declined in the last several decades; today, biologists estimate that a few hundred thousand adult females remain.

The leatherback *(Dermochelys coriacea)* is the world's most widely distributed reptile, inhabiting all of the major oceans and seas. This turtle has a leathery carapace. (The other marine turtles have hard shells.) Adults are generally 53 to 70 inches long and weigh 650 to 1,200 pounds—the largest of the sea turtles. Leatherbacks breed in the tropics, including the Caribbean; individuals range north to Newfoundland in the western Atlantic and British Columbia in the eastern Pacific. Leatherbacks can dive to depths of 1,500 feet. Heat-exchange mechanisms in the flippers, combined with the great body mass and an insulating layer of fat beneath the skin, allow leatherbacks to keep their internal temperatures several degrees warmer than the water in which they swim; this lets individuals migrate into cold regions, where they eat great quantities of jellyfish, along with squid, crustaceans, and fish. During summer, leatherbacks often are abundant in the Atlantic south of Long Island and in the Gulf of Maine.

aggressive plant. The giant reed is a native species that can outcompete other wetland plants, such as cattails and sedges, particularly if the water quality in a marsh or bog has been degraded by human activities. Bog turtles often lay their eggs in sedge hummocks; if giant reeds overtop and shade out the shorter sedges, valuable nesting habitat is lost.

Roads create barriers to the movements of turtles and many other small animals. When young turtles try to disperse from the area where they hatched, they may run into curbs or retaining walls; following along at the bases of those structures, the turtles may fall into stormwater catchment basins or drains, and perish. Many turtles, particularly females heading overland to nest, are killed by being run over by cars and trucks. The building of roads cuts up habitats into smaller and smaller areas, isolating groups of turtles from one another and preventing gene flow within a population. New highways slicing through forests or along wetlands can wipe out local turtle populations within a few years.

As a society, we must identify turtle habitats and make sure that our future developments and activities do not harm them. Turtle populations have already been dangerously compromised in many areas through habitat loss.

3
Lifestyles

M ost turtles are omnivorous, eating both plant and animal foods. Young turtles tend to be major meat eaters: They need the nutrients packed away in animal matter to grow quickly, build a hard shell, and achieve a big enough body size so they themselves are no longer easy pickings for predators—including larger turtles. Juveniles of almost all species eat many insects and other invertebrates, which are rich in protein and the shell-constructing element calcium. In some kinds of turtles, such as the cooters, found in the Southeast, adults leave their carnivorous habits behind and eat plants almost exclusively. In most species, however, individuals simply eat whatever the habitat offers and whatever their foraging techniques allow them to find—an all-inclusive strategy known as opportunistic feeding. Turtles that follow such a lifestyle are said to be generalists. Biologists do not consider generalists to have advanced as far on the evolutionary scale as the specialists that have evolved to find and process certain types of food with great skill and efficiency. But by keeping their options open, generalists are able to prosper during times when an important or a preferred food becomes scarce: They simply switch to different foods and continue filling their bellies. Writes Ronald Orenstein in *Turtles, Tortoises, and Terrapins: Survivors in Armor:* "A really aggressive and flexible generalist should be able to shift easily from food to food, from feeding technique to feeding technique, and even from habitat to habitat. An opportunistic generalist will be able to turn a wide range of circumstances to its own best advantage." As habitats are modified by plant succession, climate change, or human activities, generalists will likely have the best chance of surviving.

Orenstein points to certain populations of Blanding's turtles that dine heavily on snails, while elsewhere in the species' range crayfish are the major food item. Depending on what's available, local populations of painted turtles may be carnivorous, herbivorous, or they may eat a combination of plant and animal foods. Clearly, painted turtles are omnivorous generalists in the fullest sense. Perhaps as a result, they are highly successful as a species, with a range that extends from Atlantic Canada to Montana and from the Carolinas to Texas.

Feeding in the Water

In the water, turtles eat a variety of vegetable items: algae of many kinds, duckweed, pondweed, waterweed, water milfoil, water lily, water smartweed, wild celery, water hyacinth, water shield, watermeal, cabomba, duck potato, marsh marigold, naiad, stonewort, hornwort, cattails, grasses, sedges—the list goes on and on. One freshwater species, the Florida red-bellied turtle, eats a vegetarian diet even during the hatchling stage, and it stays with plant foods all its life. Turtles of various species eat the berries, seeds, nuts, and leaves of land plants that fall or get washed into ponds, streams, rivers, and wetlands. When aquatic turtles venture temporarily onto dry (or at least marshy) land, they may pick up vegetable items there.

In its carnivorous mode, a painted turtle will typically forage on or near the bottom of a waterway, making exploratory strikes with its head into areas likely to contain prey: niches between rocks, spaces in submerged brush or branches, interstices among stems and leaves of aquatic plants. When a leech or a crayfish or a dragonfly larva is rousted out and tries to flee, the turtle lunges at or swims after its prey. Biologists call this method of hunting the "peer-and-probe" technique, and many different kinds of turtles employ it.

Some painted turtles also use a specialized technique for collecting small food items floating on the surface of quiet water. A turtle will lift its head above the water level, then carefully open its lower jaw until the mandible barely breaks the surface of the water. As water comes rushing into the turtle's mouth, it carries in food particles. The turtle closes its jaws, constricts its pharynx, and forces the excess water out through its nostrils or its barely opened jaws, retaining the food. This form of filter feeding has been dubbed neustophagia, after the word neuston, a collective term for the tiny and, in some cases, microscopic organisms that inhabit the surface layer of a body of water. The technique resembles the filter-feeding of flamingos and baleen whales, although in turtles the behavior is less specialized and sophisticated.

Animal foods taken in aquatic habitats include snails, clams, worms, shrimp, crayfish, spiders, insects (larval forms and adults of a truly vast number of species), fish, frogs and toads (eggs, tadpoles, and adults), salamanders, snakes, birds, and carrion. In addition to actively hunting for prey, turtles lie quietly on the bottom, waiting to ambush smaller animals. The actual seizing of prey is accomplished by a sudden, powerful thrust of the head, much like a snake's strike. Some turtles also expand their throat cavities to quickly suck in volumes of water containing small animals—a method of food acquisition known as the "gape-and-suck" technique.

Many aquatic turtles, including the common musk turtle, hunt using a "peer-and probe" method: moving along on the bottom and making exploratory strikes with the head into areas likely to contain prey.

The snapping turtle is a strongly aquatic species with a highly diverse diet. These burly turtles sip down plants as small as duckweed and algae. They eat insects, from tiny larval forms to active, hard-to-catch adults. They consume fiddler crabs, crayfish, clams, water mites, leeches, tube worms, planarians, freshwater sponges, fish (of many species), amphibians, smaller turtles, snakes, birds (particularly the aquatic and semiaquatic types, such as young ducks and geese, waders, sandpipers, coots, gulls, and red-winged blackbirds), small mammals (muskrats, rice rats, and others), and carrion: pretty much any nutritious thing, living or dead, that can be caught or scavenged. A Michigan study revealed that plants made up more than a third of the volume of food consumed by local snappers, while animals amounted to more than half of the diet. In Maine, biologists determined that snappers killed and ate 10 to 13 percent of the ducklings hatched in two study areas.

Young snapping turtles hunt the shallows of lakes and ponds, walking along on the bottom and trying to catch prey. Older snappers also use the peer-and-probe method, but more often they lie in wait, relying on their rough, dark-colored shells to camouflage them against their surroundings. When a snapper detects a potential meal, the turtle unleashes a rapid head strike. The turtle may simultaneously expand its throat cavity and employ the

Some water-dwelling turtles, such as this western pond turtle, feed using a technique known as neustophagia, in which the turtle opens its jaws right at the surface so that water comes rushing in, carrying along small food items.

gape-and-suck technique. Once captured, small prey such as worms, tadpoles, or insect larvae are swallowed whole. A larger animal—a fish or a duckling—will be held securely between the snapper's hooked jaws, while the turtle's clawed forelimbs rend the hapless creature into chunks, which are then gulped down. From below, a snapper will use its jaws to grab prey floating on the surface of the water, drag the victim down, and hold on until the animal drowns. A snapping turtle was once seen lunging out at the fringe of a pond

Common snapping turtles have an extremely diverse diet that includes plants, insects, small animals such as ducklings, and carrion.

While hiding partially buried in silt or screened by underwater vegetation, the alligator snapping turtle wriggles a pink, wormlike appendage on its tongue to attract fish, which it then seizes between its jaws.

to catch a rabbit that had ventured too near the water's edge. The alligator snapper of the Deep South is even larger than the common snapping turtle and just as catholic in its feeding habits. The examination of several thousand stomachs from this species revealed the remains of fish, such as pickerel, gar, catfish, and carp; salamanders, including the large sirens and amphiumas that inhabit southern waters; snakes; small alligators; wood ducks; muskrats; raccoons; and many other animals. Persimmons, wild grapes, and acorns also are eaten. Several studies have found acorns to be the most abundant food item, by weight, in the alligator snapper's diet at certain times of the year.

The alligator snapper has a fishing lure built into its mouth: a small, pink, wormlike appendage on its tongue that it can wriggle to attract fish. When observing captive alligator snappers, scientists found that in most cases a turtle would simply close its jaws after enticing a fish inside; often the jaws clapped shut the moment that the lure was touched by the fish. Young alligator snappers do a lot of lure fishing. But as an alligator snapper matures—as its jaws strengthen and become more massive—the creature generally will switch to other foods, including smaller turtles (musk turtles are a favorite) and freshwater mussels. As a result of water pollution and siltation, native mussels are becoming increasingly scarce in many waterways, and so this food may be removed from the alligator snapper's menu. But not to worry: The alligator snapper is happy to eat the introduced, alien mussels that are proliferating in many rivers and streams. As a confirmed and flexible generalist, it is willing and able to exploit a broad range of foods.

The loggerhead musk turtle also lives in the Deep South. With its long neck and large head, it looks something like a miniature snapper. Juvenile loggerhead musk turtles prey heavily on insects. As the turtles grow, they develop heavy muscles to power their mandibles, plus an expanded crushing surface on both jaws. This enlargement seems to be an adaptation for eating mussels or for processing snails. Observers have seen loggerhead musk turtles bite down on clumps of algae, then draw their heads back while pulling the algae between their jaws, gleaning large numbers of tiny snails that were attached to the plants.

Among the map turtles, females are significantly larger than males. In Barbour's map turtle (found in the Florida panhandle and adjacent parts of Georgia and Alabama), the female is more than twice the size of the male and equipped with an immense, broad head. Male Barbour's map turtles eat mainly insects, while the females use their more-massive jaws to pulverize aquatic snails and mussels. Why are the females so much larger than the males, and why do they eat different foods? Some biologists suggest that the females, as egg layers, need the extra calcium supplied by the snail and mussel shells. Also, the differences in body and head size allow the two sexes to divvy up the food resources and avoid competing with each other in a given habitat.

As a group, the highly aquatic softshell turtles are chiefly predatory. The smooth softshell, living in the free-flowing rivers of central North America, concentrates on insects: three-quarters of its diet may consist of adult and larval forms. Other prey includes worms, snails, clams, crayfish, frogs, young birds, and small mammals; a trifling amount of plant matter is also eaten. Smooth softshells are excellent swimmers; they've been spotted catching and eating trout, extremely quick and maneuverable fish. The spiny softshell, occurring from New England west to Montana and south to Mexico, inhabits quiet waters as well as flowing ones; it eats numerous insects and broadens its diet to include mollusks, crayfish, and small fish. As with the map turtles, there may be some partitioning of the food resources between the sexes: Studies on the upper Mississippi River found that male spiny softshells ate more dragonfly larvae while females consumed more fish; in Kansas, females foraged in deep water and males fed in shallows. The Florida softshell is the third softshell species inhabiting North America. It eats many insects (more than 50 percent of the total prey items in one study) and snails (40 percent of prey). All of the softshell turtles will eat carrion, especially fish. Their sharp mandibles cut up prey with ease. Softshells are not dainty feeders: Some have been observed using their forelimbs to stuff large food items into their maws.

Feeding on Land

The familiar eastern box turtle looks placid and benign, trundling along through fields and forests. Yet to many small animals, the box turtle is a voracious predator. Box turtles eat snails, slugs, centipedes, millipedes, spiders, wood roaches, caterpillars, beetles, grasshoppers, crickets, flies, ants, termites, cicadas, maggots, and many other invertebrates. They seize salamanders and small snakes; nor would one pass up an easy meal of the eggs or newly hatched young of the smaller ground-nesting birds. Box turtles also dine on the eggs of other reptiles.

Carrion is an important dietary item, and box turtles have been seen feeding on dead ducks, herons, amphibians, mice, shrews, cottontail rabbits, and even the carcass of a cow. Box turtles also acquire food in shallow-water settings: aquatic snails, crayfish, amphibians, and assorted insects of all developmental stages.

At times, eastern box turtles eat mainly vegetarian fare. They are extremely fond of wild strawberries, blackberries, blueberries, elderberries, mulberries, grapes, ground cherries, wintergreen berries, and mayapples. A box turtle may remain in a berry patch until it has plucked every fruit it can reach and has vacuumed up all of the ones that have fallen on the ground. It's likely that box turtles are important seed dispersers for many plants. In the case of the mayapple, the eastern box turtle is the only known agent for spreading the plant's seeds; squirrels and mice eat mayapple seeds instead of dispersing them, and other mammals seem to avoid mayapples altogether, probably because the fruits contain toxins. Mushrooms are also grist for the box turtle's mill, and the species raids gardens for tomatoes, lettuce, and other vegetables.

Like the box turtle, the wood turtle feeds both on the fringes of waterways and on land. Wood turtles can switch from wild strawberries to dead fish to succulent grass to newborn mice to violets. During summer, they often move from one source of ripening berries to another. Wood turtles eat many insects, including the nymphs of the seventeen-year cicada. Other foods include leeches, slugs, snails, spiders, and ground-nesting birds. Some ecologists refer to the wood turtle as a facultative omnivore, a fancy label that means this turtle prefers animal food to plant matter. But if insects are few and far between (as during a cold, rainy spell), and if carrion is nowhere to be found, then green stuff will do the trick. Plant foods include pokeweed berries (toxic to many mammals, but apparently not to wood turtles), plantain, mullein, greenbrier, sorrel, cinquefoil, milkweed, the leaves of willows and alders, and mosses. Like box turtles, wood turtles eat wild mushrooms when those transitory foods are available.

One of the most intriguing feeding habits among North American turtles has been reported for wood turtles in both Pennsylvania and Michigan—a behavior that biologists have termed "worm stomping." A wood turtle will travel slowly through a likely habitat for earthworms, such as a low, damp area near a stream. As it moves along, the turtle will pause every few steps and stomp on the ground using its front feet. These are serious blows, audible to human observers from several yards away. A turtle will stomp for a while with one foot, then switch to the other foot, drumming at the rate of about one stomp per second. Some turtles even raise up on their legs and slam their plastrons against the ground. The impacts send vibrations through the soil, prompting worms to come wriggling to the surface; the turtles then eat the worms. Perhaps the vibrations resemble those caused by raindrops (worms commonly leave their burrows to avoid drowning when it rains) or by ground-tunneling moles, predators that earthworms try to avoid by surfacing. Biologists suggest that worm stomping may be a learned trait, since it has not been observed among wood turtles elsewhere in the species' range.

The most consistently vegetarian of the North American land turtles are the four tortoise species. In the Southeast, the gopher tortoise subsists on a wide range of plants, including legumes, grasses, asters, saw palmetto berries, papaw fruits, gopher apples, nuts, and, despite their defensive spines, prickly pear cacti and nettles. Juveniles eat essentially the same foods as adults, and if any animal matter is taken, it probably happens by accident. In the arid lands of the U.S. Southwest, the desert tortoise feeds on flowers, plantains, spurges, blazing stars, locoweeds, lupines, desert dandelions, desert mallows, cacti, and many other plants. Desert tortoises have serrated jaws that grind up plants efficiently. The digestive systems of these turtles work slowly, an adaptation that may help them survive during periods when food is scarce. Even in the summer, when desert tortoises are most active, individuals may fast for as long as a month.

Drinking

Many turtles live in aquatic environments where plenty of water is available for drinking. But for land-dwelling turtles, a source of water may be just as important as an ample food supply. Box and wood turtles often remain close to streams or ponds, where they can drink regularly. If they range away from those waterways, they may drink out of puddles. Individuals also obtain moisture from dew, and by eating fruits and other succulent plant parts.

Desert tortoises drink rainwater whenever the opportunity arises. A thunderstorm will quickly draw tortoises out of their burrows. Sometimes tortoises dig small basins to concentrate the water, so they can drink a large quantity quickly and can continue tanking up after a cloudburst ends: Basins have been observed to hold water for up to six hours. Desert tortoises have shown a weight gain of 43 percent following drinking. Tortoises also eat the pads and buds of cacti, which hold quantities of water in their tissues. When scientists studied juvenile desert tortoises in California's Mojave Desert, the young turtles were so efficient at finding and eating succulent plants that they were able to obtain twice as much water from those sources as the scientists had predicted.

Desert tortoises store excess water in their urinary bladders. When outside water sources dwindle, their bodies transfer water from the highly permeable bladder into the blood plasma. This strategy works well when the bladder's contents are more dilute than the turtle's body fluids. As waste products build up in the urine, the concentration of dissolved substances in the bladder may come to equal the concentration of dissolved substances in the blood. At that point, tortoises begin to secrete a semisolid sludge rather than liquid urine. To further conserve fluids, they may not urinate for months on end. The bladders of desert tortoises have been called "physiological canteens," and tortoises that top off their canteens by drinking deeply during rainstorms may be able to wait as long as half a year before taking another drink.

Home Ranges

Most turtles spend their lives in a limited area known as a home range. Within its home range, a turtle may frequent certain important sites, which biologists term activity centers. Home ranges can vary in size from one species to another, from one individual to another individual of the same species (males versus females, juveniles versus adults), and from one habitat or region to another. In many species, home ranges overlap, with two or more individuals using the same area of land or the same pond or portion of a water body.

Various studies of box turtles have found home ranges that were 2 to 11 acres in extent and 82 to 300 yards in diameter. Sometimes a turtle will meander about in its home range; at other times it will make a direct movement, often using a habitual travel route to shift from one activity center to another. It can take a box turtle several days or a week or longer to work its way through its entire home range. The ranges of box turtles overlap; individuals are often found together, and rarely do they show antagonism toward one another. Some box turtles, known as transients, seemingly do not occupy a home range but travel freely. When transients mate with more sedentary individuals, gene flow between neighboring populations may take place.

One study of wood turtles in Michigan pointed to fairly small home ranges. Of forty-seven turtles that scientists recaptured during the investigation, 64 percent were within 150 meters of the original point of capture, and another 32 percent were no farther than 305 meters from the first capture location. The scientists estimated average home ranges of only 0.2 to 1 acre for males and 0.6 acre to 2.25 acres for females. (Estimates of home ranges in other wood turtle populations have been significantly larger. In Algonquin Provincial Park, Ontario, biologists found individual wood turtles ranging over a couple of acres to as many as 250 acres.) Wood turtles tend to have linear home ranges that follow streams and creeks—not surprising, since these turtles frequently slip into the water to feed or cool themselves off, and many hibernate underwater. As in box turtles, the home ranges of wood turtles overlap considerably and do not seem to be defended.

Water-dwelling turtles are generally considered to be fairly sedentary. But individuals of different species can have home ranges that differ greatly in extent. The following examples all come from studies conducted on painted turtles in various parts of the species' range. In a 5-acre pond in Pennsylvania, each member of a small population ventured throughout the water body daily. In Nebraska, when shallow marshes and temporary pools began drying up in summer, painted turtles migrated overland several kilometers to more permanent waters. Turtles can and sometimes do move long distances in streams and rivers: In Saskatchewan, individual painted turtles traveled 13 to 16 miles using waterways.

With miniaturized radio transmitters becoming increasingly available and affordable, biologists are learning more about the home ranges and movements of a variety of turtles. Recent work in Tennessee reveals that bog turtles, which are quite small creatures, sometimes take impressively long journeys—one particularly active female vacated her home and traveled 2^1/$_2$ miles. Earlier studies had implied home ranges of around 3 acres for this wetlands species, and indeed, most bog turtles seem to stay within small areas, in some cases moving only a few feet per day. But at times, and for reasons that may elude scientists at present, bog turtles and turtles of other species pick themselves up and move for long distances.

Biologists have identified four main purposes for movements within a population of turtles: exploiting food sources; reproducing (locating a mate, courting, and nesting); basking; and finding places in which to hide or stay dormant over extended periods.

Activity Patterns

Most turtles are diurnal, sleeping or resting at night and becoming active during daylight hours. On land, box turtles and wood turtles spend the night resting in forms, shallow depressions that they scoop into the ground, using their plastrons; these hideouts are often masked by overarching vegetation. Desert and gopher tortoises slumber in their burrows. In brackish creeks, diamondback terrapins swim to the bottom and pass the hours of darkness buried in the mud. Some turtles are awake and moving around at night, including the musk and mud turtles, which hunt for invertebrate prey in what must amount to stygian darkness on the mucky bottoms of rivers, streams, lakes, and other aquatic habitats. In the southern part of their range, snapping turtles are active at night, but in northern areas, including Algonquin Park in Ontario, snappers do not seem to move around much after nightfall.

In the spring, after emerging from hibernation, turtles crawl or swim about, looking for potential mates and then courting and breeding. Turtles can be active for much of the day during this feverish season; sometimes the urge to mate even overcomes the need to eat and restore nutrients used up during the winter hibernation. In summer, as days lengthen and temperatures rise, turtles concentrate more on feeding, basking, and resting. A study in Putnam County, Florida, found that gopher tortoises basked 76.4 percent of the time, walked about 16.5 percent, fed 4.1 percent, mated 1 percent, and nested 1 percent.

Most North American turtles are active at temperatures between 68 and 86 degrees F (20 to 30 degrees C). Some turtles, such as the land-dwelling tortoises, can function in warmer settings: The normal body temperature of an active gopher tortoise approaches 95 degrees F. At the other end of the scale is Blanding's turtle, which ranges farther north than any other turtle species on the continent. In the northern part of their range, Blanding's turtles become active several weeks earlier in the spring, and remain active several weeks later in the fall, than do snapping turtles and painted turtles in the same habitats. Another turtle notable for remaining functional in the cold is the spotted turtle. One that was found crawling through shallow water beneath the ice had a cloacal temperature of 37.4 degrees F—the coldest temperature ever measured in an active turtle.

Because turtles are unable to manufacture heat through internal body processes, as mammals do, their body temperatures—and their activity levels—depend on the temperature of their surroundings.

During spring, summer, and fall, aquatic turtles move from cool areas into warm zones, and vice versa, when they want to warm up or cool down. The young of many aquatic species show a preference for sun-warmed shallows, where their metabolic rates are sustained at a heightened level: With their systems running at full throttle, the juveniles can eat and process a lot of food, helping them to grow more quickly.

Basking

Basking is an important behavior that allows turtles to efficiently raise their body temperatures. Both land- and water-dwelling species engage in this common reptilian practice.

At night, turtles gradually take on the ambient temperature of their surroundings. By morning, they can be very sluggish. The quickest way for a turtle to jump-start its system is to crawl into the sun. Whether lying in an opening in the woods, floating on the surface in shallow water, or perching on a streamside log or rock, a basking turtle will try to position its body to intercept the maximum amount of sunlight possible. Many turtles have dark shells; the dark coloration conveniently soaks up heat from the sun.

When a turtle exposes itself to the sun and radiant heat begins warming its carapace, temperature sensors in the nervous system cause an increase in blood flow. Experiments conducted on painted turtles and box turtles have shown that the hypothalamus, an area in the brain stem, is particularly important in temperature regulation. When a turtle basks, blood passing through vessels near the skin and just beneath the shell quickly begins shuttling heat to the body's core. If the turtle suddenly moves into a cooler microhabitat—let's say it hears a raccoon prowling along on the stream bank, and dives back into the water—its blood vessels constrict, holding heat inside the body. Turtles are very good at regulating their internal body temperature. Young spiny softshells can warm up twice as fast as they cool down. Under some conditions, desert tortoises can heat up ten times faster than they chill.

If it feels secure in its choice of a basking site, a turtle may lie resting flat on its plastron, stretching its neck and limbs far out of the shell and even spreading out its toes in an effort to soak up sunlight. Basking gets the animal ready to use its muscles and venture out into the environment to find food. After a turtle has filled its belly with bugs or carrion or grass, it may go lie in the sun again, since the enzymes in its digestive tract work best at higher temperatures. In the laboratory, scientists found that recently fed females basked longer than recently fed males, and individuals of both sexes basked longer than their unfed counterparts. Plants being harder to digest than animal matter, vegetarian feeders, such as the cooters, particularly need to bask.

Basking confers additional benefits. It helps turtles synthesize vitamin D, important in shell growth. Basking lets the skin of aquatic turtles dry out, which may make leeches and other external parasites let go or fall off. Basking suppresses the growth of algae. (Algae tufting a turtle's shell can slow the reptile down in the water, cause the shell to deteriorate, and spread diseases that can weaken or kill an individual.)

Some turtles bask frequently; others do so less often. The mud and musk turtles of Family Kinosternidae bask rarely. A number of the species in Family Emydidae, also known as the semiaquatic or pond turtles, spend much of each day basking; however, they do not bask when the air temperature is lower than the water temperature. Map turtles are particularly well-known as baskers. Map turtles live in large rivers and lakes. Soon after they emerge from hibernation in the spring, the sexes get together and mate. (Some map turtles also mate in autumn.) Another springtime priority, especially for female map turtles, is to find places to get out of the chilly water and lie in the sun. In northern areas, map turtles may be so keen to start basking in springtime that they clamber onto ice floes to sun themselves. Warming their bodies promotes the production of eggshells containing the embryos developing in the females' reproductive systems. Basking helps map turtles and other turtles get their eggs laid earlier in the year, which in turn makes it more likely that their hatchlings will grow large and strong enough to make it through their first winter.

Traditional basking sites may be used for generations. A naturalist friend of mine once went back to a small lake in Georgia where, as a youth, he had spent many hours watching the several species of turtles that basked along the shore. In the intervening years, people had built houses around the lake and, to clean up their properties, had carted off logs, brush, and other unsightly debris, creating a shoreline barren of basking sites. Despite looking around for several days, my friend saw no turtles in what once had been a thriving habitat.

Turtles of many different species often converge on prime basking sites. If space is limited, they jostle one another in trying to stake out the best spots on rocks, logs, snags, and shoreline areas. Big turtles shoulder aside smaller turtles; smaller turtles climb onto the backs of larger ones. Turtles may threaten each other with open mouths or even bite in an attempt to claim or defend an excellent site. Some turtles—usually younger, smaller ones—may be forced to use poorer or more difficult spots, such as tree trunks angling up steeply from the bank. (Musk turtles sometimes ascend small trees that slant out over the water, climbing as high as 6 feet. Some have fallen into canoes when the boats, in passing, startled them off their perches.) In the false map turtle, individuals often bask side by side, orienting their bodies so that the tail of one turtle is alongside the head of its neighbor, or so that their posteriors are together— positioning strategies that minimize aggressive face-to-face interactions.

When basking, water-dwelling turtles are temporarily out of their element, a situation that makes them extra wary and hard to approach. Softshell turtles usually keep their heads pointed toward the water, which lets them make a rapid escape if danger threatens. Many basking turtles hold their eyes closed, so that direct sunlight does not dry out sensitive eye tissues and perhaps to exclude damaging ultraviolet rays. These turtles listen carefully for potential predators. When turtles bask en masse, it always seems that one or more in the group will have its eyes open. If that turtle glimpses any movement, it quickly slides into the water, causing an instant panic among the remaining baskers.

Where basking sites are limited, turtles jostle each other aside and sometimes even climb onto one another's backs to claim a place in the sun, as these western painted turtles are doing.

People who float in canoes down rivers are sometimes startled by the sight and sound of a gang of turtles scrabbling off a rock or log and splashing into the water. Tortoises living in hot, dry habitats also bask, particularly on mornings following chilly nights. In summer, they may keep their basking sessions short to prevent overheating. Desert tortoises bask at the entrances of their burrows, into which they can retreat if they get too hot. When basking, a tortoise may let the sun shine onto its carapace while holding its head and neck out of the light.

Beating the Heat

During hot weather, a land-dwelling turtle may bask in the morning, feed for an hour or so, and then retreat to a cool, moist place during midday. It may lie in the shady shallows of a lake or stream, rest inside the burrow of some other animal, or dig down into decaying leaves or the rotting wood of a log or stump. Some terrestrial turtles enter the water and bury themselves in the mud. Biologists term this heat-avoidance behavior estivation. Aquatic turtles also estivate by digging into the mud if their home ponds or marshes start drying up. Turtles may estivate for a few hours, a few days, or even several weeks. While estivating, they may become torpid. Cooler weather or a period of rain may draw them out into the habitat again.

If for some reason a desert tortoise cannot retreat inside its cool burrow, it will try to find another shady spot. If shade is unavailable, it will spread its own saliva on its head, neck, and front legs; as the saliva evaporates, the tortoise is cooled. The ornate box turtle of the Plains states uses both saliva and urine to promote this evaporative cooling. Sometimes a land-dwelling turtle or tortoise will tip over onto its back, either by accident or through aggressive contact with another turtle. If an overturned turtle ends up lying in direct sunlight and can't right itself, it may die from overheating.

Hibernating

Many North American turtles hibernate to escape winter's chill. Some swim to the bottoms of rivers, streams, lakes, or ponds, where they dig down into sand or mud or lie resting in the layer of water, directly above the bottom, that generally remains unfrozen. Their brain activity dwindles, and they move very little. Depending on how far north they live and how long the winter lasts, turtles may stay dormant for as long as six or even seven months.

All turtles that scientists have studied can obtain oxygen when underwater, some more effectively than others. When hibernating, common map turtles cluster in oxygen-rich areas of streams and rivers, where they take in oxygen through their skins. Softshell turtles have gill-like structures inside the throat, which give off carbon dioxide and absorb oxygen. While lying on a pond or river bottom, red-bellied turtles open and close their jaws up to six times per minute, cycling water through their throat cavities and gleaning oxygen from it. Some snapping turtles and painted turtles winter in stagnant waters, where they make do with little or no oxygen. Turtles that hibernate while dug into a lake or stream bottom, or buried deeply in soil on land, also can withstand anoxic or near-anoxic conditions.

Oddly enough, some of the most strongly aquatic turtles sometimes winter on land. Three mud turtle species winter either on the land or in the water. In the northern part of their range, chicken turtles vacate their ponds in favor of terrestrial sites where they dig down into mud or damp sand. Turtles of several species occasionally winter in groups, including map turtles, bog turtles, spotted turtles, and wood turtles. As many as seventy wood turtles have been found hibernating together in a beaver pond. These turtles cannot be getting together to share body heat, for the simple reason that a dormant turtle gives off very little heat energy. More likely, they find a particular site attractive for one reason or other—for instance, the water maintains a high dissolved oxygen content. Another possible advantage to overwintering in a group is that individuals can find mates more readily in the spring.

Southwestern Utah is at the northern limit of the desert tortoise's range. There, tortoises hibernate in large communal dens, some dug as deep as 33 feet into gravel banks. Up to twenty-three tortoises have been found in such dens. Most communal dens are ground squirrel burrows that have been enlarged, over time, by generations of desert tortoises; some scientists believe the burrows may be thousands of years old. Farther south, in Arizona, desert tortoises dig their own, smaller hibernacula. These burrows are sited well above the floor of an arroyo, out of the area where cold air would pool, and on a south-facing slope. A burrow typically extends far enough into the soil so that the rear of the tortoise's shell remains even with the arroyo wall. The burrow protects its occupant from the wind, and on clear days the afternoon sun falls upon the tortoise's shell, providing radiant heating.

In the Southeast, when gopher tortoises enter dormancy in the fall, they void the contents of their intestines. Emerging from their dens in the spring, they eat some of their own dried droppings to restore the bacterial flora in their digestive systems.

Some eastern box turtles hibernate in the mud of pond and stream bottoms. But most spend the winter on land, digging themselves in beneath rotting leaves and other debris or tucking themselves away inside stump holes or mammal burrows. Some box turtles move as far as a mile to seek out a favored hibernaculum. An individual may hibernate in the same spot several years in a row, and several box turtles may hibernate together. If the ground is soft, a box turtle may dig itself in deeper as winter temperatures fall; some go as deep as 2 feet. As winter wanes and the frost line recedes, the turtle gradually digs its way upward. In an Ohio study, biologists found that the body temperatures of hibernating box turtles sometimes dipped below freezing, yet the turtles survived. Turtles do not have a natural antifreeze in their bodies, as some other animals do. Most turtles seem able to withstand some slight freezing, but if they become frozen more thoroughly, they will die.

The heart of a hibernating turtle may beat only once every five to ten minutes. In the laboratory, painted turtles held underwater at a temperature of 37.4 degrees F have a metabolism operating at only 10 to 15 percent of normal. Over time, however, even a radically throttled-back metabolism will produce the waste product known as lactic acid. Painted turtles deal with lactic acid by neutralizing it with calcium and magnesium carbonate, drawn largely from the bones and the shell. The turtles release the mineral ions into the bloodstream to buffer some of the lactic acid. Additional lactic acid is taken up into the skeletal system, where it is stored mainly in the shell. Other than turtles, scientists know of no other animals that can directly incorporate lactic acid into their bones.

Most young turtles hatch in late summer or early fall. Juvenile snapping turtles, Blanding's turtles, and the young of many other species enter streams or lakes and spend their first winter in dormancy at the bottoms of those water bodies. Baby box turtles, mud turtles, and painted turtles overwinter in the ground. After hatching, ornate box turtles and yellow mud turtles instinctively tunnel down through the bottom of the nest chamber to get below the frost line.

In the North, painted turtle hatchlings do not burrow down into the soil; instead, they ride out the winter in a nest that their mother may have dug no deeper than 5 inches below the ground's surface. Young painted turtles have a physiological defense that provides them with some protection against freezing: Their skin includes a dense layer of lipids, particularly on the head and forelimbs—the parts of a turtle that, unprotected by the shell, are most vulnerable to cold. This water-insoluble layer may prevent frost crystals from penetrating a hatchling's skin and, once inside the body, setting up a chain reaction that would cause body fluids to crystallize into ice. When snows pile up, the baby turtles are well insulated, but in years with little or no snow hatchlings may freeze to death.

Predators

A biologist working in Fakahatchee Strand State Preserve in southern Florida told me about a time he went wading in a swamp. As he made his way through the murky, waist-deep water, he kept probing in front of his feet with a machete, testing the bottom for alligator holes. Alligators dig such holes as a means of concentrating water during the dry season; the biologist did not want to step in one accidentally and go in over his head. His machete hit something hard, and up through the greenish water came floating a large snapping turtle. The turtle was dead. A semicircle of deep puncture wounds marked the top of its shell. The wounds described the broad radius of a large alligator's jaw. The biologist surmised that his machete had struck the turtle and dislodged it, either from the bottom of the pond or—and he considered this to be of equal likelihood—from an alligator's mouth. (Fortunately for him, alligators are rarely aggressive toward humans.)

In the southern states, alligators take many turtles of various species, both large and small. Some scientists believe that the thick, highly domed, hard-to-crush carapace of the Florida red-bellied turtle evolved in response to predation by alligators. In aquatic habitats, the snapping turtle and, in the Deep South, the alligator snapping turtle are both major predators on many other species of turtles—seizing, crushing, and consuming both juveniles and adults.

In many cases, turtles find their prey by following olfactory signals; they also use those signals to evade predators. One experiment focused on the way razorback mud turtles and stripeneck mud turtles (both species of the South) behave in the presence of an alligator snapper. A scientist first placed the mud turtles in a tank in which one specific zone contained water from a separate tank where river cooters and sliders had been living. (River cooters and sliders do not attack or kill adult turtles of other species.) The mud turtles wandered freely through the tank, including the cooter/slider zone. Then the scientist put the mud turtles in a tank with an area of water from a tank housing an alligator snapper. The mud turtles avoided the snapper-tainted water. Clearly, chemical cues prompted both mud turtle species to stay away from a known and feared predator. Turtles thwart predators by avoiding detection in the first place and by fleeing as quickly as they can when an enemy approaches. Because turtles can pick up low-frequency vibrations, such as those caused by footfalls, they are often put on alert well before a large land predator gets close. A box turtle may freeze in place, shutting itself inside its shell and hoping that its shell markings will blend it in with the sun-dappled forest floor. Other turtles are also well camouflaged, both on land and in the water, by the colors and textures of their shells. When a tortoise pulls back into its shell, its head and face are concealed behind its folded forelegs, which are large, stout, and armored with hard scales; at the back, only the tortoise's tough-soled feet are exposed to a predator's attack.

As well as a protective shell, turtles have some other defensive weapons they can use to ward off enemies. When threatened, snapping turtles make themselves look imposing by raising up the back half of the body while opening the mouth and hissing. If a predator tries to circle, the snapper spins around quickly to face its foe. When attacked, a snapper will strike with open mouth, bite hard, and hang on determinedly. Both the common snapping turtle and the alligator snapping turtle have extremely powerful jaws. Many people have reported snapping turtles biting through sticks, tool handles, and other sturdy prods. Some scientists and naturalists came to doubt this notion, thinking it an exaggeration. Recently, turtle biologist Peter Pritchard tested the concept by teasing a 165-pound alligator snapper with a broom handle. The turtle seized the stick between its mandibles and bit through it cleanly.

Many turtles use their jaws to defend themselves. The softshell turtles have extremely sharp mandibles that can deliver a painful, shearing bite. They also have long and flexible necks, letting them keep an enemy at a distance. Softshells and many other turtles have sharp claws, with which they can rake an attacker. When stressed or frightened, a turtle may squirt the contents of its excretory system out through the cloaca, a ploy that may put off some predators. Musk turtles bite and scratch vigorously when handled and they also release a musky fluid from a pair of glands located on each side of the body beneath the border of the carapace; phenylpentanoic and phenylalkanoic acids make the musk extremely pungent. Snapping turtles also can release a potent, putrid scent.

On land, adults of the smaller turtle species fall prey to black bears, hogs, coyotes, foxes, dogs, raccoons, skunks, opossums, otters, bald eagles, and the larger hawks. Thomas Tyning, a naturalist with the Massachusetts Audubon

Society, once spotted a young red-tailed hawk dive to the ground and then flap up to a tree limb, clutching a small box turtle in its talons. The hawk occasionally pecked at the turtle with its beak, but eventually it dropped the reptile. When Tyning examined the turtle, it seemed not to have been harmed by the hawk; a turtle of a different species, unable to withdraw its limbs fully or clamp itself tightly inside its shell, might have been wounded or killed by the attack.

Turtles are often found with mutilated or missing limbs and damaged shells. During a long-term study in Michigan, 12.5 percent of marked wood turtles lost limbs to predators, and 2 percent ultimately came to be missing two limbs. The recapture rate for wounded turtles was much lower than it was for uninjured ones, suggesting that a turtle who has lost a limb is considerably less likely to make it from one year to the next. Still, some individuals with missing limbs were recaptured several years in a row, proving that some wood turtles are able to shrug off serious injuries, at least for a while.

Many scientists judge the raccoon to be the top predator on turtles in North America. Raccoons are intelligent, adaptable omnivores whose numbers have increased dramatically in the last century, largely because of human development and settlement patterns. (Ecologists refer to predators that have been helped by human activities as subsidized predators.) Raccoons thrive in the fragmented habitats of urban, suburban, and farming areas; they also inhabit wetlands and adjacent dry lands, prime feeding and breeding habitats for many species of turtles.

A raccoon can deliver a quick immobilizing bite to the head of an unsuspecting turtle, and then feed at will. Raccoons have been known to kill and eat adult spotted turtles, bog turtles, wood turtles, and diamondback terrapins (particularly nesting females of the latter species). The raccoon is considered to be the top predator on painted turtles of all ages, rangewide. In Virginia, in the early spring, biologists found where raccoons had dug adult snapping turtles out of shallow mud and then eaten the cold, lethargic reptiles (wisely starting in from the rear). In the winter, box turtles, if they have neglected to bury themselves deeply enough in the ground, may be unearthed and eaten by raccoons as well as other predatory mammals. In Florida, raccoons have learned to dig hatchling gopher tortoises out of their burrows, a practice that has wreaked havoc on some local populations.

Raccoons also destroy a great many turtle nests. After female turtles lay their eggs, they fill in the holes with dirt and, in almost all species, crawl away without a backward glance. Raccoons may start digging up and eating the eggs almost immediately. During some years, raccoons can destroy 100 percent of the clutches laid by a single species of turtle in a given area. When biologists removed raccoons from a study area in Iowa, no fewer than seven turtle species showed significant increases in egg-laying and hatchling success.

Turtle eggs feed a horde of other animal opportunists. When diamondback terrapins emerge from tidal marshes to dig their nests on barrier dunes, gulls fly over the dunes or perch on utility poles, watching and waiting. A gull will land near a laying female, eat two or three eggs, and fly off with one in its beak; even as these depredations take place, the female terrapin may continue laying.

Coyotes, gray foxes, red foxes, badgers, skunks, opossums, ground squirrels, red and gray squirrels, chipmunks, woodchucks, crows, grackles, wild turkeys, kingsnakes, garter snakes, copperheads, bull snakes, hognose snakes—all have been spotted rifling turtle nests. Ants and crabs can also get into the nests and dismantle the eggs. Some scientists have estimated that an individual female turtle may produce a successful nest only once in every ten years.

It turns out that even plants prey on turtle eggs in some environments. In a study conducted on barrier island dunes, five of twenty nests of the diamond-back terrapin were infiltrated by the fine rootlets of beach grass. Several of the eggs actually burst when the rootlets entered their shells. In a separate study, scientists collected terrapin eggs and injected them with radioactive isotopes of cesium, selenium, manganese, and iron; then they reburied the eggs in their original nest. Beach grass attacked some of the eggs, and within forty-five days the isotope markers showed up in the roots and shoots of grass plants more than a foot away from the nest. Ecologists suspect that beach grass absorbs key nutrients from terrapin eggs as a means of surviving in the mineral-deficient soils of sand dunes.

Since young turtles have soft shells, they are easy pickings for many preda-tors. In addition to most of the nest robbers listed above, hatchlings also attract the attention of feral cats, mink, rice rats, herons and other wading birds, rap-tors (including hawks, eagles, kites, and vultures), fish (gar and largemouth bass take many juvenile turtles), bullfrogs, and crabs. Ravens are important subsidized predators in some areas, including urban and suburban zones in southern California and in the state's highly agricultural Central Valley. There, raven populations have increased anywhere from ten- to more than seventy-fold in the last several decades, with particularly high densities of these intelli-gent, omnivorous birds living along power lines and roadways, where they prey heavily on baby desert tortoises.

Beyond a doubt, humans are the greatest enemies that turtles face today. In much of the world, including parts of the United States, people have long killed turtles for their meat. The land-dwelling gopher tortoise of the Southeast was once known as "Georgia bacon" and "cracker chicken," because it formed an important part of the diet for rural families; as a result, populations of this turtle were wiped out in many areas. In the late nineteenth and early twentieth centuries, diamondback terrapins were considered to be gourmet food, and humans hunted them until few could be found, particularly near cities of the eastern seaboard. Fortunately, local populations of diamondback terrapins have rebounded across much of the species' range. On the opposite coast, peo-ple formerly ate western pond turtles, causing the species to decline. Snapping turtles have long been favored as food: Nowadays, "terrapin soup" is usually made with the meat of snappers, which are usually caught on baited hooks. In some areas, overharvesting has caused the number of snappers to dwindle.

Dangers abound in human-altered habitats. In brackish waters, diamond-back terrapins may enter submerged crab pots; unable to escape, they drown. On land, turtles of numerous species fall into concrete drainage culverts and can't escape. Farming operations destroy many turtles, and uncountable numbers are run over by cars and trucks. Lawnmowers kill small terrestrial types, such as box turtles and wood turtles. People also capture turtles, either to keep them as pets or to sell them, sometimes peddling them illegally to collectors in foreign countries: box turtles, wood turtles, spotted turtles, bog turtles, desert tortoises, gopher tortoises, and other attractive species are frequent victims of this exploitation. Because turtles can take several to many years to mature sexually, removing even a few adults can seriously jeopardize local populations.

Parasites and Diseases

Turtles that spend most or part of their annual cycle in the water are apt to pick up leeches, bloodsucking annelid worms up to 2 inches long. Most snapping turtles have leeches, which often attach to the skin at the limb sockets; some snappers play host to hundreds of these parasites. Musk and mud turtles are often leech-infested. Turtles that do not hibernate beneath sand or mud, such as wood turtles and common map turtles, may be plagued with leeches year-round; even as the turtles lie dormant at the bottom of a stream or pond, the leeches continue feeding on their blood. More than half of the wood turtles monitored in a West Virginia study carried leeches.

Leeches may let go or die when turtles leave the water and bask. Map turtles allow grackles to land in basking areas and peck at leeches clinging to their skin, and minnows have been seen cleaning leeches from wood turtles in the water. At times, turtles bury themselves in ant mounds; a female snapping turtle recovered from an ant mound in Michigan was the only one of thirty-nine studied to be leech-free. Land turtles can also play host to ticks, which attach to their soft parts, and flesh fly larvae. Mosquitoes sometimes take blood meals from turtles, and in so doing may introduce viral infections and internal parasites.

Captive native turtles can catch diseases from other captive turtles, which may have been brought to North America from distant lands. If people then return their sick pets to the wild, exotic diseases may be introduced to local populations.

In the American Southwest, desert tortoises have contracted a highly contagious illness known as upper respiratory tract disease, or URTD. The disease is caused by a microorganism known as a mycoplasma, believed to have arrived in this country in infected imported turtles. URTD can be quite virulent: In a 1-square-mile area in the Desert Tortoise Natural Area in southern California, tortoise numbers plummeted from 204 counted in 1982 to only 13 found ten years later.

Tortoises in Nevada's Las Vegas Valley and in Utah and Arizona have also been infected. URTD has set back efforts to restore desert tortoises to habitats from which they have disappeared: When biologists relocate tortoises to new areas, the stress of the move can make the tortoises more susceptible to the disease. URTD has also stricken some gopher tortoises in Florida.

4

Reproduction

Thomas Tyning is a naturalist on the staff of the Massachusetts Audubon Society. In his book *A Guide to Amphibians and Reptiles,* he recalls how he heard a loud splashing coming from a beaver pond on an early spring afternoon. "It took several minutes of watching through binoculars to identify the cause of the commotion—two snapping turtles, locked together, tumbling over and over in the shallow water." The turtles were both males, engaged in a struggle to establish dominance. At one point during their set-to, which lasted for forty-five minutes, "the two rose vertically out of the water," Tyning writes. "They were belly to belly, with their necks straining and their front feet clasping each other. They were literally standing up on the bottom of the pond, then slowly they toppled."

Rarely are the activities associated with turtle reproduction quite as dramatic as the battle Tyning observed. In the main, turtles beget their generations quietly and unobtrusively—as they have been doing since the earth was a much younger place.

Mating

Most turtles start looking for mating opportunities soon after they emerge from hibernation in spring. But turtles' bodies actually set things up well in advance of this stirring of reproductive activity. During the preceding summer, when food was plentiful and warm temperatures supported a heightened level of physiological activity, male turtles produced sperm, and females began forming eggs. Winter brought matters to a temporary halt, as the turtles, hidden away beneath leaf duff or soil or tucked into the muddy bottoms of ponds, slowed their metabolic rates drastically to survive the cold.

After the ice melts from ponds and streams and after the frost leaves the ground in spring, males start searching for receptive females. Females do not seem to actively search out males but remain in their usual habitats and let the males come to them. Both lengthening days and warmer temperatures are key factors in initiating breeding. Rising water temperatures goad female musk turtles and snapping turtles to resume their reproductive cycles. During years when there are more warm days in early spring, Blanding's turtles start breeding earlier, with the result that females nest earlier in the year than usual.

In searching for mates, males may wander overland or swim about for considerable distances. When checking out the neighborhood, a male may run into other males of the same species. Male snapping turtles often behave aggressively toward one another; as Tyning describes it, "individuals face each other in shallow water and lunge forward in a slow-motion, sumo-wrestlerlike encounter." They may kick, bite, and scratch. "These encounters may cause cuts and bruises but have rarely been recorded as ending with the death of either of the combatants," Tyning writes.

At the other end of the size scale, male bog turtles threaten each other by making a direct advance while extending the head with the mouth open. When an aggressor is almost touching a rival, he will partially withdraw his head and tilt his carapace forward by raising the hind legs and lowering the front legs; competitors may push, shove, and occasionally bite at the opponent's head and legs. In many other species, fights between males are ritualized affairs that do not cause serious injury to either foe. Sometimes posturing alone does the trick: A male wood turtle may drive off another male by advancing ominously with his mouth wide open.

Male tortoises are well-known for their aggressive behavior toward fellow males and also toward females that are potential mates. Combat between male tortoises is known as "jousting." A male tortoise possesses a gular projection, a sturdy extension on the front of the plastron just below the chin. When two males meet, they circle each other, looking for a chance to attack their opponent's flank. Ramming into one another repeatedly, the males try to use their gular projections to lever their rival over onto his back. Once overturned, a tortoise will be out of the chase for females until he can get himself righted, which may take quite some time. In what is a humorously human-appearing behavior, male tortoises sometimes use their hind feet to kick sand into their rivals' faces. When a male finally gets together with a female, the male will bob his head up and down—a fairly common mating behavior among male turtles, and one that may help an individual pick up scent. Then, as an invitation to copulate, the male tortoise will ram his shell into the female's flank—somewhat more gently than he would ram another male.

Initially, most turtles probably recognize potential mates by sight. Scientists using decoys have shown that a male who is ready to mate will chase after any moving object of approximately the correct size. After getting close

Male tortoises often fight or "joust" during the breeding season. Rivals circle each other; one may then advance quickly and use his gular projection—a sturdy extension of the plastron—to try to lever his opponent over onto his back.

to another turtle, a male will carefully sniff at the stranger to determine whether the turtle is a female of his own species. The nose being the keenest sensory organ in turtles, an error in distinguishing between species is very unlikely. Even underwater, turtles recognize their own kind easily by smell. In many turtles, the anal glands produce highly odiferous secretions that may be important in bringing the sexes together.

Depending on the species, there may be little in the way of courtship. In mud and musk turtles, softshell turtles, and some other species, the act of mating resembles forcible rape. But in most turtles, at least some interplay occurs between the sexes, often including stylized movements and behaviors that may act as a barrier to prevent breeding between different species. If a male does not behave toward a female in a certain manner, the mating process will be short-circuited and sexual intercourse will not take place.

In wood turtles, the male stands in front of a potential mate and extends his head and legs to display the bright orange skin on his neck and forelimbs. As well as striking a handsome pose, a male wood turtle will pursue a female and grab at her shell with his feet. In common snapping turtles, both males and females take in air, then release bubbles through their nostrils while facing each other underwater.

Like most North American turtles, painted turtles mate in the water. The male, much smaller than the female, slowly swims after his mate-to-be. When he finally overtakes her, the male swims on past and then turns to face the female. Using the backs of his foreclaws—which are much longer than the female's claws—he strokes her head and neck. If receptive to the male's over- tures, the female uses her own foreclaws to stroke the male's outstretched forelimbs. Between periods of stroking, the male may swim away, apparently trying to entice the female to follow him. This behavior may be repeated sev- eral times. Finally, the female sinks to the bottom of the creek or pond. The male mounts her from behind and copulates with her.

The males of many North American semiaquatic turtles stroke or tap the faces of females during courtship. In a number of species, this behavior is enhanced by the males' elongated front claws. Male sliders, chicken turtles, and false map turtles do not stroke or tap the female or even touch her with their long claws. Instead, they vibrate their claws next to her head. The male river cooter sports claws that are straight and extremely long, like a bunch of small nails. He swims above his chosen mate, holds his foreclaws on each side of her face, and rapidly vibrates these ornamental features, each vibratory burst lasting about half a second. If unreceptive, the female will try to outswim the male or dart beneath an obstruction to displace him. Females of other species may say "no" rather more emphatically. If a male smooth soft- shell sniffs at a basking female, she may turn and snap at him, her sharp mandibles inflicting a bloody wound on the edge of his leathery carapace.

In turtles, the male's penis is composed of spongy connective tissue. Usu- ally it lies flaccid inside the cloaca, the opening in the base of the tail from which urine and feces are expelled. When the male is sexually aroused, the penis fills with blood, becoming enlarged and erect; emerging from the cloaca, it projects backward. Since male turtles are often smaller than females of the same species, and because turtles' shells make for a somewhat remote coital embrace, male turtles have relatively large penises for their overall body size. During copulation, the penis must be inserted into the female's cloacal open- ing. To abet this penetration, the male uses his tail as a guiding mechanism. He may also hook his front claws over the front rim of the female's carapace, while gripping the trailing edge of her plastron with his back claws. Another male mating behavior is to bite at the female's neck: This makes her retract her head, which in turn causes her to extend her rear end, exposing her cloaca.

By mating in the water, males can somewhat overcome gravity, which oth- erwise might make them slide or fall off the females' backs. In a number of species, the plastron of the male is concave, letting it fit more securely over the female's carapace and helping the male remain in place during copulation.

Although considered one of the semiaquatic turtles, the eastern box turtle is largely terrestrial and mates on land. A box turtle has a high, domed shell, a shape that makes it particularly difficult for the male to mount the female. When mating, the male works himself up into a standing position behind the female. To keep from falling over, he hooks his rear claws behind the rear mar- gin of the female's plastron, whereupon she raises the rear lobe of her plastron to clamp his feet in place. The male tilts farther back until his shell rests on the ground. He plants his feet on the ground to improve his balance and shifts

The males of many water-dwelling turtles, such as this river cooter, have extremely long claws on their front feet, which they use to stimulate females during courtship.

forward to insert his penis. After he penetrates the female, gravity sometimes wins out, causing the male to fall over onto his back. If the female crawls away, he may be dragged along behind. After the two part, he may be unable to right himself; male box turtles have died because they were lying in loose sand and could not get themselves turned over again.

In turtles there is no pair bond between the sexes, and mating is random. After the sex act, males and females go their separate ways. A female may mate with several males to ensure fertilization, and a male will try to mate with as many females as possible to advance his own genetic material. DNA fingerprinting has shown that some clutches of eggs have two or more fathers. Sperm may remain viable in a female's oviducts for a long time: Captive female box turtles and diamondback terrapins have laid fertile eggs four years after any male contact. There are important advantages to being able to store sperm: A female can time the fertilization of her eggs so that the resulting hatchlings leave the nest at the optimal time for their survival; and she can lay several clutches following a single mating.

Eggs

Turtles do not give birth to live young. Like birds, most snakes, crocodiles, and lizards, turtles lay eggs containing embryos well supplied with food and water and protected from the environment by an external wrapper. Of all the creatures listed above, turtles give the least care to their eggs once they've laid them. Mother turtles basically consign their reproductive future to the earth by burying their eggs and then walking away and letting the sun incubate the clutch. This lack of brood care has been interpreted as evidence that turtles are very primitive creatures indeed.

Compared with the eggs of fishes and amphibians, those of reptiles are quite complex. Inside the egg, the embryo is connected by an umbilical stalk to the primary food supply, a yolk sac whose golden yellow matter is a rich blend of sugars, starches, fats, and proteins. Blood vessels carry the nutrients via the umbilical stalk to the developing embryo. The embryo is surrounded by the amniotic sac, a fluid-filled chamber that cushions the embryo from shock: In essence, a baby turtle develops in an aquatic environment. The amniotic sac and the yolk are both housed within the allantois (the term comes from a Latin word meaning sausage-shaped), an envelope that arises from the embryonic alimentary canal. Waste products from the embryo pass into the allantois, which expands as the embryo grows and the yolk dwindles. Another membrane, the chorion (derived from a Greek word for gut), surrounds the allantois, amniotic sac, yolk sac, and embryo. The chorion contains a layer of albumin, also called egg white, which supplies the embryo with water. The chorion is permeable to oxygen and carbon dioxide, as is the eggshell. In turtles, the eggshell is composed of crystals of aragonite, a form of calcium carbonate.

Turtle eggs can be spherical to ovoid to elongated in shape, depending on the species. The shell may be flexible and tough, or hard and brittle. Many river turtles lay flexible, soft-shelled eggs, while the hard-shelled ones are laid by some aquatic species (including softshells and musk and mud turtles) and by tortoises in arid habitats. In general, leathery or parchmentlike eggs with little calcium in the shell require nests having a higher humidity or soil moisture level than do hard, heavily calcified eggs. The amount of moisture that reaches an egg can affect the size of the hatchling, with smaller hatchlings coming from nests that are lacking in moisture. Too much moisture can be detrimental as well: If a river rises and floods a turtle's nest for too long a period, embryos will not receive the oxygen they require to develop, and they will suffocate and die.

The number of eggs laid at any one time depends mainly on the size of the female. Larger, more mature females produce greater quantities of eggs, while smaller females deliver smaller clutches—a concept that holds true both across species lines and within a given species. In turtles, egg size is relatively consistent between species. For example, a 2-foot-long alligator snapping turtle lays a spherical egg roughly $1^{1}/2$ inches in diameter. A spotted turtle, which is about 4 inches long, lays an egg that is approximately $1^{1}/2$ inches long by $3/4$ inch wide. The alligator snapper generally lays twenty to fifty eggs per clutch, while the diminutive spotted turtle lays only three or four eggs.

Generally a larger, more robust female will lay slightly larger eggs than a smaller female of the same species. The bigger the egg, the larger the yolk sac and the larger the resulting hatchling—with larger hatchlings having a heightened chance of surviving.

Digging a Nest

Some turtles put very little effort into digging a nest. The loggerhead musk turtle scrapes out a shallow hole, often against a rock or stump. Bog turtles sometimes place their eggs in sedge tussocks; while laying, the female separates the blades of sedge using her hind feet, or she simply tunnels through the vegetation, leaving eggs in her wake.

The majority of North American turtles bury their eggs in the ground beneath soil or sand, or hide them in rotting wood or plant matter. Aquatic species clamber onto land to accomplish this task, with some individuals moving a mile or farther away from the water before settling on a nest site. A female may try several sites before finding a satisfactory one. Female diamondback terrapins touch their snouts to the sand when looking and may check out as many as ten places before finally starting to nest.

The females of some species clear out a sizable area, pushing aside any vegetation or loose soil that might clog the nest chamber; lying in this preliminary excavation (sometimes called a body pit), they then dig the actual nest. The eastern mud turtle starts out using her forelimbs, slinging dirt to the sides until she is almost out of sight; then she switches to her hind legs and digs the egg chamber. Typically, a female turtle excavates a flask-shaped chamber, using alternating strokes of her hind legs; the depth of the nest depends on how far down her legs can reach. While working, she may void the contents of her bladder on the earth to make the digging easier. It's interesting to note that desert tortoises, whose front limbs are highly adapted for digging burrows, turn around and use their hind legs to dig their nests.

As she lays her eggs, a female may use her hind feet to arrange them within the nest chamber. Several layers of eggs may be deposited, with a small amount of dirt pushed in on top of each layer. After she has laid her clutch, the female uses her hind legs to shove dirt in on top of the eggs. Then she smooths out the site, pressing down on the nest with her plastron or dragging the plastron across the filled-in area, so that the site ends up looking much as it did before the eggs were laid. Female red-bellied turtles stand up high on their legs and then drop down heavily, tamping the dirt. Some females urinate on the sand or dirt as they repack it. It usually takes a turtle an hour or two to dig a nest, lay eggs, and cover the nest up—and sometimes much longer. Spotted turtles in Illinois have taken up to twelve hours to complete a nest.

Blanding's turtles and false map turtles may start digging during daylight on cloudy days. Female common snapping turtles often nest during the day, usually in early morning or late afternoon. Diamondback terrapins are also daytime nesters. But most turtles nest at night, probably because it's harder for predators to detect them in the dark than during the light of day. Some turtles return to nest in the same spot year after year.

Females nest in places that are likely to receive the optimal amount of sunshine. If a nest gets too hot, the embryos will die; if it doesn't warm up sufficiently, the eggs will develop too slowly or will fail to develop. Large turtles, which have correspondingly long legs, may locate their nests in the open, burying the eggs deeply enough that they won't overheat. Smaller turtles that can excavate only shallow nests may choose spots nearer to grass or other plants, so that their nests receive shade for part of each day. Some aquatic turtles, including softshell turtles and diamondback terrapins, nest in open sandbars. The eggs of these turtles are adapted to develop even under the extremely hot temperatures that can build up in sand exposed to direct sunlight. Some turtles construct decoy nests. A cooter may build three nests; she will lay most of her eggs in one nest and only a few eggs in the other two nests. The primary nest is carefully covered and smoothed over, while the decoy nests are covered minimally or not at all. A predator may easily find and eat the eggs in the decoy nests, and miss the larger primary nest. Florida red-bellied turtles sometimes lay their eggs in the rims of alligator nests, perhaps to gain protection against mammalian nest predators. After striped mud turtles lay their eggs, they may not head straight back to the water, instead burying themselves in soil or rotting vegetation. Biologists have speculated that the females may lie in these humid sites waiting for rain, to avoid becoming dehydrated. An alternate theory holds that the females pause on land so that rain will wash away any scent trail that a predator might follow back to find the nests. The yellow mud turtle actually digs herself into the soil on top of her eggs—maybe to protect them from predators or perhaps to help keep the level of soil moisture high. This behavior comes the closest to parental care of offspring shown by any North American turtle.

Most female turtles use their hind feet to scoop out a nest chamber in the ground. Then they lay eggs in the chamber, cover the clutch with dirt or sand, and walk away, leaving the eggs to be incubated by the sun's warmth.

Turtles of several species—including the common snapping turtle, Blanding's turtle, and spotted turtle—nest just once each year. If a predator discovers the nest and eats the eggs, a year's reproductive potential goes down the drain. A female desert tortoise may hedge her bets by nesting twice: once in late April or early May, and a second time in late May or early June. Female painted turtles may nest three to five times annually. A number of turtles lay multiple clutches; several species in Florida lay up to six clutches per year—essentially nesting year-round. Spreading out the nesting activity increases the odds that at least some clutches will not be destroyed by predators or disabled by floods or other environmental conditions. Smaller turtles may lay multiple clutches simply because their bodies cannot hold many eggs at one time. A female mud turtle, for instance, may lay only two or three eggs per clutch, but she may bring forth three clutches per nesting season.

TSD and GSD

Beginning in the 1960s, herpetologists made a series of startling discoveries regarding the developmental processes leading to the sex of turtle embryos. The scientists found that, in a number of species, the temperature at which eggs are incubated determines the sex of the hatchlings. They named this phenomenon temperature-dependent sex determination, or TSD. TSD is exhibited by most species in Family Emydidae (the most abundant group of turtles in North America) and in tortoises.

Here's how it works: If an egg's average temperature stays below a certain threshold, or pivotal temperature, during the period when the embryo's reproductive organs are developing, the hatchling will be male. If the temperature remains above that threshold, the hatchling will be female. Should a clutch of eggs be incubated close to or at the pivotal temperature, a mixture of males and females will result.

An alternate TSD pattern has been recognized in snapping turtles and in some of the musk and mud turtles. Their eggs have two pivotal temperatures, one low and the other high. Males are produced when eggs are incubated at a temperature between the two thresholds. But if temperatures hold above the upper threshold or dip below the lower one, the resulting hatchlings will be female.

In both forms of TSD, different species show different pivotal temperatures. In the painted turtle, the pivotal temperature is 81.5 degrees F (female embryos above that value, males below it). In the gopher tortoise, the pivotal temperature is between 84.2 and 89.6 degrees F. Timing is crucial: Laboratory experiments have shown that TSD operates only during the middle third of the incubation period, the time when the embryo's sex becomes fixed. Later in the cycle, fluctuations in temperature will have no effect on gender. Temperatures during the middle third of incubation do not have to be constant, but they must be above or below the threshold for at least part of the day.

Other factors also come into play in TSD. If an egg is situated in the top layer of several layers in a nest, it may receive more radiant heat from the sun and may therefore yield a female hatchling. An egg in the bottom layer, where ambient temperatures remain cooler, may hatch out as a male. Nests in shady areas may produce mostly males, while those in sunny spots yield females. Studies of map turtle nests found that the majority of the young emerging from any given nest were likely to be of the same sex. Perhaps female turtles, during the course of their annual nesting cycle, create some male nests and some female nests, leading to a balance of males and females in the population.

Turtles that rely on TSD lack sex chromosomes. But other turtles do possess sex chromosomes: They exhibit genetically based sex determination, or GSD. So far, scientists have discovered that the sex of softshell turtles and the wood turtle depend solely on the embryos' individual chromosomes and not on temperatures in the nest. Some species, including the striped mud turtle, seem to show both TSD and GSD. In the alligator snapping turtle, there does not seem to be any temperature that will cause all of the eggs in a clutch to develop as males. Writes Ronald Orenstein in *Turtles, Tortoises, and Terrapins: Survivors in Armor:* "This suggests the possibility that at least some of its eggs—perhaps as many as a third—may be destined to be female no matter what their incubation temperature."

Scientists are not sure exactly how TSD works. Nor have they determined what advantages it may bestow. Some herpetologists suggest that TSD may somehow lessen the chances of inbreeding in years to come, when hatchlings have matured. Or TSD may affect the ratio of males to females: Species exhibiting TSD generally produce more females than males, which can be advantageous, because a single male is capable of fertilizing more than one female. TSD may have conferred evolutionary advantages on certain species in the past. Clearly it has played some as-yet-undetermined role in the evolution of turtles and their distribution in different environments. But today it may be detrimental to some species. As temperatures rise at an unnaturally high rate due to global climate change, TSD may cause the structure of turtle populations to change drastically. For example, if all the nests in an area or a region produce only males or only females, local populations may be wiped out. Biologists are monitoring turtles to keep track of this worrisome possibility.

Exiting the Shell

A baby turtle can take a long time to develop from an embryo in a newly laid egg to a hatchling ready to struggle out of the nest and into the world. In North America, some of the slowest-developing eggs belong to the desert tortoise, which hatch three to four months after they were laid. Box turtle eggs normally take seventy to eighty days to hatch. Snapping turtle eggs require seventy-five to ninety-five days, with northern populations taking longer than southern ones. In the laboratory, wood turtle eggs have been induced to hatch in only forty days when held at temperatures above 86 degrees F; in nature, about two and a half months is more usual. In general, the length of the incubation period depends on soil temperature, which is in turn affected by exposure to sun and shade, air temperature, soil characteristics, and rainfall.

A baby turtle comes equipped with a caruncle, or egg tooth, a horny projection at the tip of the snout. The youngster uses this temporary bump (it falls off after a week or so) to slice open or puncture the eggshell, which, by hatching time, has become quite thin, much of its calcium having been diverted to the growing embryo. A young turtle will work its forelimbs back and forth and make stretching movements, further weakening the eggshell. Periods of struggling and resting alternate; a juvenile may take from several hours to several days to exit the shell.

Hatchlings are good diggers. If the outside environment is warm and inviting, they will quickly tunnel upward through the soil and emerge. But if the ground above is frozen, or baked into a hardpan by the sun, baby turtles will remain in the nest chamber for some time. Hatchlings may even dig downward to escape frost, a behavior documented in yellow mud turtles and ornate box turtles. Juveniles of some species, including red-eared sliders, hatch out but then stay dormant in the nest through their first winter, finally emerging in the spring when sunlight warms the ground.

Some scientists have suggested that it may require the combined work of a whole brood of hatchlings to break through the soil compacted above a turtle nest. But baby turtles in a given nest may not all hatch in unison. In a study of Blanding's turtles in Michigan, all hatchlings emerged on the same day in 70 percent of fifty-nine nests that scientists monitored; in the other 30 percent of nests, hatchlings freed themselves over a span of up to four days. In nests of gopher tortoises in Florida, hatchlings took as many as sixteen days to make their way out of the same nest.

After hatching, a young turtle stretches out its body, which was curved to fit inside the eggshell; quickly it becomes 10 to 25 percent longer than the egg was. When some young turtles leave the nest, they carry with them food reserves in the form of the dwindled yolk sac, about the size of a pea or a bean and remaining attached to the center of the still-soft plastron by the umbilical stalk. A youngster can draw on the remaining nutrients in the yolk sac for a week or longer, until the structure finally shrivels and falls off. Many young desert tortoises emerge from the egg with a substantial yolk sac. Rather than beginning to feed, they instead start to dig a burrow, where they can hide from predators and insulate themselves from the harsh desert environment.

Many young turtles must travel a long way from the nest site to a suitable habitat. They use their senses to pick up cues: Aquatic turtles listen for the sound of rushing water, or look for areas of uniform brightness that may signal an expanse of water. Many turtles simply head downhill, generally the correct direction to follow for arriving at the water. The hatchlings of some species, including Blanding's turtle and the wood turtle, appear to follow scent trails laid down by other hatchlings. Some juveniles move quickly to their chosen habitat, while others embark on a slower, more cautious route. As they travel, they may stop periodically and hide beneath the leaf litter, in clumps of moss, and inside the burrows of small mammals. This leisurely trip may help the youngsters imprint on and remember their surroundings.

Since they are small, slow-moving, and have soft shells, hatchlings are easy pickings for a variety of land and water predators. (For a full description of predation, see chapter 3, "Lifestyles.") Many young turtles are adorned with

Juvenile turtles, such as this wood turtle, must overcome many challenges, obstacles, and dangers before they grow large enough to become reproducing adult members of the population.

bright colors, something that seems counterintuitive in a creature that wants to avoid being noticed by a hawk or fox or snake. Some animals use brilliant colors to advertise the fact that their bodies contain poisonous compounds, but juvenile turtles—at least those in North America—do not seem to produce such toxins. Hatchlings, however, have sharp claws and strong jaws that they do not hesitate to use in self defense. Largemouth bass are highly predatory fish. Most, however, tend to avoid hatchling turtles, probably because the young turtles, when seized, scratch and bite determinedly: Researchers have watched large bass take turtles, then spit them out again. Most of the aquatic turtles that have bright colors display them on the plastron, rather than on the carapace, which is usually dull. Perhaps the bright undersides warn off fish swimming below a hatchling, while the drab carapace hides its wearer from other predators, such as birds, that strike from above. A small percentage of turtles survive for a year after hatching. In the gopher tortoise, only about 6 of every 100 hatchlings make it to age one, and for several years thereafter more than half of all remaining juveniles perish.

Becoming an Adult

Because they're so vulnerable when young, it behooves turtles to get big as quickly as they can. During the first several years of their lives, most juveniles concentrate on eating highly nutritious foods, including insects and other invertebrates, that spur growth. Turtles of many species show substantial increases in size and weight during their early years. And it's not just to thwart predators: The larger a turtle becomes, the better able it is to survive environmental stresses, such as extreme cold and prolonged drought.

Turtles grow more slowly than mammals and birds do. As with all the reptiles, they have low metabolic rates and reduced energy requirements compared with warm-blooded creatures. Turtles can survive long periods without food and, in some cases, without water. But the trade-off for having a slow metabolism is that a turtle does not reach sexual maturity for a number of years. In turtles, sexual maturity is linked more to body size and condition than to age: Once a turtle achieves a certain size, it can then afford to divert energy and resources to the production of eggs or sperm.

In general, male turtles mature at an earlier age than females. Slow-growing species such as gopher tortoises and desert tortoises reach maturity at ten to more than twenty years of age. Eastern box turtles mature at five to ten years. Female painted turtles can breed when six to ten years old, males when three or four. In the smooth softshell, males are ready to breed in their fourth year, but females are unable to do so until they're about nine years old. Alligator snapping turtles grow rapidly until they are eleven to thirteen years of age, when they become sexually mature; growth slows dramatically after about age fifteen.

Once a female turtle matures, she has the potential to live for many years and to lay many clutches of eggs. She may not nest every year, however, if the resources necessary for reproduction are not available. Over her lifespan, she will see good years and lean years; times when food is abundant, and other periods when food is scarce and long winters or extended drought force months spent in dormancy. When times are tough, a female turtle may reabsorb ovarian follicles that do not ovulate, recycling the nutrients they contain in a process known as atresia.

5

Species Accounts

This chapter includes an illustrated field guide to twenty-two of the most common turtle species in North America. Below is a quick page locator for the species included. Fuller descriptions including size, habitats, feeding habits, and nesting are found in this section. Tips on markings and aspects such as dark color in older turtles, observing individuals, and correlating different species with habitats are also described in individual species accounts.

Snapping Turtle
(Chelydra serpentina)

Snapping Turtle Family
(Chelydridae)

About the name: "Snapping" refers to this powerful turtle's propensity to snap at prey and at enemies. *Chelydra* is Greek for "water serpent," and *serpentina* is Latin for "snakelike"; both words identify the snapping turtle's long neck. This turtle is also called snapper, and some rural folk know it as loggerhead because of its large head.

Size at maturity: large. Adults are typically 8 to 14 or more inches from the front of the carapace to the back. Most weigh 10 to 35 pounds, but old individuals can approach 20 inches in length and weigh 75 pounds.

Distribution: Snapping turtles occur from Atlantic Canada west to southeastern Alberta and south to Florida and Texas, from sea level to about 6,000 feet. The species is also found in parts of Central America and northern South America. Snapping turtles have been introduced in many areas outside their natural range.

Description: Easy to identify, thanks to the large size, big head, and hooked upper jaw. The long tail (in adults, as long as the carapace; in juveniles, longer than the carapace) has a row of sawtooth projections on top. The upper shell can be tan, brown, olive, or almost black, with three keels running lengthwise (these may be worn-down on older specimens) and a serrated edge. The plastron is yellowish, cross-shaped, and small, affording little protection to the undersides.

Key identifiers: large size, big head, rough shell.

Habitat: Snappers live in lakes, reservoirs, ponds, rivers, streams, marshes, swamps, and estuaries; along the coast, they inhabit salt marshes and sometimes venture into saltwater bays. The ideal habitat is a shallow freshwater swamp or lake margin with a muddy or sandy bottom, submerged logs and brush, and abundant aquatic and emergent plants.

Feeding habits: These turtles walk about slowly in search of prey or lie buried in the muck in ambush. More than half of the diet consists of animal items, including insects, crayfish, snails, worms, fish, frogs, salamanders, small turtles, snakes, birds (such as ducklings), small rodents, and carrion. Snappers also eat many plants, including algae.

Distinctive behaviors: Snappers are most active at dawn and dusk, and at night. While they do not bask as often as many other turtles do, snappers sometimes lie on fallen tree trunks and limbs; they also float in the water with the upper shell exposed to the sun's warmth. Relatively tolerant of cold conditions, they may crawl along on the bottom of their watery habitat beneath the ice in winter. They hibernate underwater, burying themselves in muck or beneath logs or plant debris, and emerge again in April or May. Snapping turtles are famously pugnacious and defend themselves vigorously when threatened. Their sharp jaws can deliver a wicked bite.

Reproduction: During the spring breeding season, males may wrestle with each other, perhaps to establish social dominance. Mating takes place in the water. Gravid females leave the water and move inland to lay eggs. Females deposit their eggs in nests that they dig in loose soil or sand, gravel banks, sawdust piles, earthen dikes, pond and lake margins, and along roadsides and railroad beds. A female typically will lay twenty to forty eggs, although clutches containing more than one hundred eggs have been found. The eggs are white and about the size and shape of Ping-Pong balls. The temperature of their surroundings helps determine the sex of the developing embryos. Eggs hatch after three to four months.

Population trends: Snapping turtles are adaptable and widespread. Their population is generally healthy, although in some areas people have captured many snappers for their meat, depressing local numbers. ("Terrapin soup" is often made from the flesh of snapping turtles.)

When to look: Snappers can be spotted in lake and pond shallows, basking in the sunshine of early spring. Males may battle during the April–May breeding period, splashing loudly. You are most apt to see a snapper when the females leave the water to nest, around the middle of June.

Similar species: The closely related alligator snapping turtle (*Macrochelys temminckii*) is even larger than the common snapping turtle; its range centers on Louisiana, Mississippi, and Arkansas and extends east to Florida and north along the Mississippi River to Illinois and Iowa.

Common Musk Turtle
(Sternotherus odoratus)

Musk and Mud Turtle Family
(Kinosternidae)

About the name: "Musk" describes the strong-smelling secretions released by glands beneath the carapace. *Sternotherus* comes from the Greek *sternon,* "chest," and *thairos,* "hinge," and refers to the hinged plastron; *odoratus* commemorates the bad-smelling musk. These turtles are also known as stinkpots, skillpots, and stinking jims.

Size at maturity: small. Adults' carapaces are 2 to 4$^1/_2$ inches long, rarely 5$^1/_2$ inches.

Distribution: Common musk turtles occur from New England south to Florida, and from southern Ontario, Michigan, and Wisconsin south to eastern Texas and the Gulf states. (Four other musk turtle species—razorback, loggerhead, stripeneck, and flattened—inhabit parts of the Southeast.)

Description: The smooth, high-domed carapace is grayish brown to black, often tufted with algae. The small-ish plastron is yellowish or brown, with an inconspicuous hinge. The chin and throat are adorned with two pairs of barbels, and two yellow stripes run from the end of the snout to the neck. Males have long, thick tails that end in a hard, sharp point, plus a deep notch at the back of the plastron; females have smaller tails, smaller heads, and no notch in the plastron.

Key identifiers: small size, hinged plastron, two pale lines on head, barbels on chin and throat.

Habitat: Common musk turtles thrive in rivers, streams, lakes, ponds, swamps, sloughs, and canals; they favor still or slow-moving water and a muddy bottom. They prefer shallows but have been found in water more than 25 feet deep. Individuals live in areas usually less than 5 acres in extent.

Feeding habits: Small musk turtles eat algae, aquatic insects, and carrion, with a decided emphasis on animal matter; larger individuals may consume a wide range of foods, including plants, snails, clams, crayfish, leeches, tadpoles, and frogs. Poor swimmers, musk turtles often feed on the bottom, walking along underwater with the head extended, using a "peer-and-probe" technique to explore crevices between rocks when searching for prey. Musk turtles are known for taking worms attached to fishermen's hooks, and many are injured that way.

Distinctive behaviors: When handled, musk turtles often emit a foul yellowish liquid from glands near the bridge linking the carapace and plastron. This musk may have evolved as a deterrent to predators, or it may be involved in courtship. Biologists know little about the overwintering habits and site preferences of musk turtles; some individuals use muskrat lodges, but most probably sink themselves in debris on the bottoms of water bodies. Adults can live at least twenty-eight years in the wild, and some may reach fifty.

Reproduction: In the South, musk turtles breed from February to May; in the North, breeding occurs about a month later. Mating takes place in the water. A male follows a female, nipping at the edge of her shell and at her head and neck. When a receptive female stops, the male grabs onto her shell using all four feet while resting his head on hers. Three to eight weeks after mating, females venture onto land to nest. They lay their eggs in shallow nests made by scraping away leaf mold and rotting wood. A typical clutch contains two to five eggs; sometimes several females use the same nest site, intermingling their eggs. Some females lay several clutches in a year. The eggs hatch after two to three months, with the sex of the young determined by nest temperatures.

Population trends: Musk turtles dwindle when humans drain wetlands and locate development too close to rivers, streams, and ponds.

When to look: Musk turtles are active mainly at night and can be spotted soon after sunset when they feed along the margins of ponds and lakes. Choose a calm night (so the wind doesn't ripple the water) and direct a strong light into the water.

Similar species: The eastern mud turtle (*Kinosternon subrubrum*) is a similar size and shape, but has two hinges on the plastron, instead of the musk turtle's single hinge, and lacks the musk turtle's yellow facial stripes.

Eastern Mud Turtle
(Kinosternon subrubrum)

Musk and Mud Turtle Family
(Kinosternidae)

About the name: "Mud" identifies the substrate on the bottoms of the streams and ponds where this turtle dwells. *Kinosternon* comes from the Greek *kineo,* to move, and *sternon,* breast, describing the doubly hinged plastron; *subrubrum* combines the Latin words for "under" and "red" and refers to a mottled pattern on the plastron of hatchlings.

Size at maturity: small. Adults are 2³/₄ to 4 inches, with a few individuals exceeding 4¹/₂ inches.

Distribution: The eastern mud turtle is found from Long Island, New York, south to northern Florida and northwest to Kentucky, Indiana, and Illinois. Taxonomists recognize two additional subspecies: the Florida mud turtle, in peninsular Florida; and the Mississippi mud turtle, living along the Gulf Coast west to Texas and north into Oklahoma. The three subspecies, or races, interbreed where their ranges meet.

Description: When viewed from above, the carapace is oval. Smooth and lacking a keel, it is yellowish to olive or black. The yellow to brown plastron is equipped with two transverse hinges, one in front of and the other behind a fixed bridge that spans the plastron across its center. The skin is brown or olive. Some mud turtles have yellow markings on the head. Males have longer, thicker tails than females, and the males' tails end in a hard, nail-like tip.

Key identifiers: small size, rounded shell, double-hinged plastron.

Habitat: Mud turtles like slow-moving water and a muddy bottom with plenty of vegetation. They are found in ditches, sloughs, rivers, streams, ponds, marshes, bayous, and cypress swamps. Some individuals live in tidal marshes in coastal areas and on barrier islands, where they tolerate brackish conditions well.

Feeding habits: Mud turtles eat aquatic insects, mollusks, crayfish, carrion, and vegetation. Smaller individuals concentrate on small insect forms (such as dragonfly nymphs), algae, and carrion. Mud turtles feed mainly on the bottoms of waterways, but they also take insects and other prey when they venture onto land.

Distinctive behaviors: Mud turtles usually rest by day and do their foraging under the water at night. They bask, but not as frequently nor for such long periods as many other turtles. If their watery habitat dries out, mud turtles may burrow into the muddy bottom and estivate, or they may climb out of the water and spend time on land. In northern areas, they hibernate by digging into the soft bottoms of waterways, in rotten logs or piles of leaf litter and other debris on land, and in shallow burrows excavated in the soil. In southern climes, mud turtles may stay active for much or all of the year.

Reproduction: Mud turtles mate in the spring, from mid-March through May. Most matings happen in the water, although some take place on land. Females nest mainly in May and June, on open ground not far from the water. They dig egg chambers in sandy, loamy soils, and they also deposit their clutches in heaps of vegetable debris and rotting wood. Most clutches have three to five eggs. After about three months the eggs hatch, in late August or September. Sometimes the young turtles stay in the nest through the winter and emerge the following spring.

Population trends: Good habitats can hold lots of mud turtles: a ten-year survey found an average annual population of 371 in a 25-acre area in South Carolina. Habitat loss and degradation threaten local populations of mud turtles, as they do many other turtle species.

When to look: Mud turtles are most active at night, when it can be very difficult to spot them in the shallow waters where they do most of their feeding. A strong light shone from the pond or stream edge may reveal a swimming or foraging turtle.

Similar species: Musk turtles (*Sternotherus* species) are similar in size and shape, but have a single hinge on the plastron rather than the mud turtle's pair of hinges. Also, musk turtles sport yellow facial stripes, which are absent in most mud turtles.

Yellow Mud Turtle
(Kinosternon flavescens)

Musk and Mud Turtle Family
(Kinosternidae)

About the name: "Mud" denotes the muddy bottom in many of the aquatic habitats where this turtle lives. *Kinosternon* comes from the Greek *kineo,* to move, and *sternon,* breast, and refers to the species' doubly hinged plastron; *flavescens* is Latin for yellowish.

Size at maturity: small. Adults are 4 to 5 inches long, rarely 6 inches.

Distribution: The yellow mud turtle is a resident of the Midwest and Southwest. It is found in western Illinois and adjacent Iowa and Missouri in the alluvial plain of the Mississippi River. Farther west, it occurs from northern Nebraska south through western Kansas and eastern Colorado to Oklahoma, Texas, New Mexico, Arizona, and northern Mexico. Herpetologists recognize three subspecies or races.

Description: In the more common western race, the carapace is broad, smooth, somewhat flattened, and colored olive to brown; the scutes are outlined with dark borders. The plastron is yellowish to brown, with two transverse hinges. The skin is yellow or grayish yellow: Look for the yellowish chin and throat. (Yellow mud turtles in and around Illinois have dark carapaces and dark gray or black skin.) The jaws are hooked, and the feet are webbed. Males have longer, thicker tails than females, and the males' tails end in a hard, pointed tip.

Key identifiers: flattened carapace, yellowish chin and throat, double-hinged plastron.

Habitat: This grassland and desert species occupies quiet-water habitats including rivers, creeks, lakes, ponds, sloughs, backwaters, swamps, sinkholes, reservoirs, and cattle tanks. The habitat usually has a mud or sand bottom. In northern Nebraska, the yellow mud turtle requires sandy soil where it can dig beneath the frost line in winter.

Feeding habits: Yellow mud turtles eat snails, earthworms, insects, and other invertebrates, along with tadpoles and carrion. They also eat some plant matter, including duckweed.

Distinctive behaviors: Mainly active during the day, yellow mud turtles may also move around at night. They like to bask. In the heat of midsummer they estivate, mainly on land, burying themselves in sandy soil; rainy weather brings them out again. Sometimes these turtles move overland between bodies of water, a habit that has helped them colonize ponds scattered throughout their range. In winter they hibernate by burrowing into natural depressions, such as stump holes, and beneath brush piles and rotting logs; often they dig themselves deep into sandy soil. Some individuals hibernate in mud at the bottoms of ponds. Under severe conditions, these turtles can remain dormant for up to two years, drawing on lipids stored in the body.

Reproduction: Yellow mud turtles mate in the water. The male uses his claws to grasp the edge of the female's carapace; he further secures himself on the female's back by inserting his sharp-tipped tail under the edge of her carapace. In May or June, the female moves away from the water up to 600 feet to a sparsely vegetated, south-facing slope, where she digs herself down several inches into the sandy soil before excavating an egg chamber. One to nine eggs are laid. Unlike most other female turtles, the female yellow mud turtle may stay with her clutch, burying herself on top of her nest and remaining in this position for one to more than thirty-eight days; her presence may reduce predation on the eggs and help retain soil moisture in the nest. The eggs hatch from July to October; heavy rainfall seems to stimulate hatching. In some regions, the juveniles remain underground until the following spring, when rains, coupled with warming soil temperatures, cause them to emerge.

Population trends: The yellow mud turtle is very rare in Iowa. In Illinois, where the species is considered endangered, much habitat along the Green, Illinois, and Mississippi Rivers has been destroyed by dredging and lock and dam construction; other threats include lowered water tables and intensive farming practices. Farther west, the yellow mud turtle remains abundant.

When to look: During rainy periods, yellow mud turtles are most apt to wander on land. Rainfall stimulates their movements, most of which take place at night.

Similar species: Musk turtles (*Sternotherus* species) are similar in size and shape, but have a single hinge on the plastron rather than the mud turtle's pair of hinges.

Spotted Turtle
(Clemmys guttata)

Box and Water Turtle Family
(Emydidae)

About the name: This turtle is named for the polka-dot spots on its carapace. *Clemmys* is from the Greek *klemmys,* a tortoise; *guttata* is Latin for "spotted."

Size at maturity: small. Adults' carapaces are 3^1/$_2$ to 4^1/$_2$ inches long, rarely 5 inches. Females average slightly larger than males.

Distribution: Spotted turtles occur from Maine to Florida on the Atlantic coastal plain. They also live as far west as Michigan and Illinois.

Description: The dark, almost black carapace is scattered with small yellow spots. The number of spots (in some cases, 100 or more) and their location vary between individuals. (Naturalists often sketch the patterns so they can recognize individual turtles later.) The spots are transparent areas in the scutes that overlay yellow pigment beneath. The plastron is yellow in young turtles; it darkens with age, and in older turtles it may be entirely black. Yellow or orange spots also mark the head, neck, and limbs, while the lower surface of the limbs may be orange or salmon. Males have brown eyes and a tan chin, and females have orange eyes and a yellow chin, characteristics that often can be seen through binoculars.

Key identifiers: small size, yellow spots on dark background.

Habitat: Spotted turtles live in ponds, slow-moving streams, shallow marshes, bogs, swamps, ditches, and wet meadows, with a soft bottom and aquatic vegetation. At times, and in some parts of the species' range, individuals spend a significant amount of time on land.

Feeding habits: Spotted turtles are omnivorous scavengers. Aquatic grasses and filamentous green algae are common plant foods; animal matter includes aquatic insect larvae, slugs, snails, worms, tadpoles, salamanders, fish, and carrion. Hatchlings are more carnivorous than adults.

Distinctive behaviors: Spotted turtles are among the most cold-adapted of turtles. In spring they often emerge from hibernation when ice still rims the ponds. They bask on logs and tussocks on sunny days. If frightened, they may abandon these sites, slip into the water, swim to the pond bottom, and burrow into mud or vegetation. During summer's heat they often enter cool streams and crawl into underwater vegetation or inside muskrat dens. In some years, individuals carry their estivation through fall and go right into hibernation; thus, they remain inactive from around July until the following March or April, the time at which spotted turtles resume their activity in spring. (Normally, spotted turtles begin hibernation in September.)

Reproduction: During the spring mating season, males actively chase females; sometimes competing males bite at each other. Mating takes place in the water. Around June, females leave their aquatic habitats to find nest sites: meadows and fields and areas along roadsides that are exposed to full sunlight. Typically starting in the evening, the female will dig a shallow nest chamber 2 or $2^1/_2$ inches in depth. In it she lays an average of three or four eggs—fewer than many other species. After scooping soil back over her clutch, she flattens the nest by pressing her plastron down on top of it. Droughts sometimes kill the developing turtles. The eggs hatch after approximately eleven weeks. Hatchlings are about $1^1/_8$ inches long.

Population trends: In many areas, populations are falling as habitats are fragmented or destroyed by development and large-scale agriculture, and as wetlands are drained or degraded. Adult spotted turtles are removed from the population when people collect these handsome reptiles for the pet trade. Many females are killed by cars and trucks while crossing roads during the nesting period.

When to look: The best time to observe spotted turtles is in early spring, when they are actively feeding, basking, and breeding, and before thickening pond vegetation obscures them or hot weather sends them into dormancy.

Similar species: Blanding's turtle (*Emydoidea blandingii*) also has yellow markings on a dark shell and, in the Upper Midwest, may occupy the same habitats as the spotted turtle. Blanding's, however, is larger (5 to 10 inches) and has a hinged plastron and a bright yellow throat and neck, features that the spotted turtle lacks.

Bog Turtle
(Clemmys muhlenbergii)

Box and Water Turtle Family
(Emydidae)

About the name: "Bog" indicates the wetlands habitat that this species requires. *Clemmys* is from the Greek *klemmys,* a tortoise; *muhlenbergii* honors Heinrich Mühlenberg, first president of Franklin College in Lancaster, Pennsylvania, who, in the late 1700s, discovered the first, or "type," specimen of this turtle.

Size at maturity: small. This is the smallest North American turtle, with a carapace only 3 to 3¹/₂ inches long (the record is 4¹/₂ inches). Males average slightly larger than females.

Distribution: The bog turtle has a discontinuous range, whose major part extends from western Massachusetts and Connecticut and southeastern New York south to New Jersey, Delaware, Pennsylvania, and northern Maryland. Separate colonies exist in western New York, western Pennsylvania, and western North Carolina.

Description: The most striking aspect of this small turtle's appearance is an orange, yellow-orange, or reddish blotch on each side of the head. (In some individuals, the blotch is broken into two parts.) The carapace is dark brown or black, with a low keel running along the midline from front to back. The plastron is also dark in color.

Key identifiers: small size, orange blotch on head.

Habitat: Bog turtles live in spring-fed sphagnum bogs, tamarack and spruce swamps, and marshy meadows, from sea level to more than 4,000 feet in the southern mountains. They require clear, slow-moving waterways with a muddy bottom. Grasses, sedges, alders, swamp orchids, skunk cabbage, and various ferns are common in the open-canopy bogs and fens inhabited by *Clemmys muhlenbergii*.

Feeding habits: Bog turtles feed both on land and in the water. They eat many insects, including caterpillars, crickets, beetles, and caddis fly larvae, and also consume frogs, slugs, salamanders, earthworms, millipedes, carrion, and plants.

Distinctive behaviors: Bog turtles are active mainly during the day. In the morning, they leave the cover where they rested overnight and spend time basking before setting off in search of food or mates. They rest during the hottest hours and may estivate during the hottest days of summer in wet areas and tunnels that are partly or completely filled with water; some individuals estivate in muskrat bank burrows or lodges. From around October into March or April, bog turtles hibernate in the soft bottoms of streams and brooks; in sedge tussocks; at the bases of stumps; or in the burrows of muskrats and other rodents. Clusters of more than 140 individuals have been found overwintering in the same general area.

Reproduction: Bog turtles mate in early spring. Females nest from May to July, usually three to four weeks after mating. They dig shallow nests in pastures, soft soil, and sphagnum moss; some do not build a nest at all but simply drop their eggs while crawling through sedge tussocks. Although the typical clutch contains three eggs, some adult females produce only a single egg.

Population trends: This is our rarest turtle. The most severe population threat is habitat loss, some of it caused by plant succession but most of it resulting from humans draining, polluting, or developing wetlands (including very small wetland areas). The illegal collecting of adults, to be sold or kept as pets, can eradicate local populations or drastically reduce their reproductive potential. The alien plant purple loosestrife, introduced from Europe, has ruined some bog turtle habitats by choking out native plants, particularly sedges. Bog turtles are classified as "threatened" on the U.S. Endangered Species list, and many states also bestow "endangered" status on this turtle.

When to look: Bog turtles are most active in the spring. Look for them in the morning, when they often bask on sedge tussocks and other habitat features.

Similar species: The spotted turtle (*Clemmys guttata*) looks somewhat similar and also inhabits wetlands. Its dark carapace, however, lacks a keel; it has many yellow spots; and it does not have the bog turtle's colorful head markings.

Wood Turtle
(Clemmys insculpta)

Box and Water Turtle Family
(Emydidae)

About the name: "Wood" refers to the woodland areas this turtle inhabits. *Clemmys* is from the Greek *klemmys,* a tortoise, and *insculpta* recognizes the sculpted appearance of the wood turtle's shell.

Size at maturity: medium. Adults are $5^1/_2$ to 8 inches long, with some individuals exceeding 9 inches. Males are slightly larger than females.

Distribution: Wood turtles live from Nova Scotia west across southern Quebec to eastern Minnesota. The species' range extends south to northern Virginia in the East, and an isolated population occurs in northern Iowa.

Description: The carapace is covered with raised scutes shaped like irregular pyramids. The scutes are gray-ish brown with darker brown markings; those edging the rear of the shell are serrated, and they flare outward noticeably in juveniles and females. The plastron is yellow, with oblong dark blotches at the outer rear corner of each scute. The head is black. The skin is dark brown, marked with yellow, orange, or red on the throat, neck, tail, and especially the underside of the forelimbs—hence the old name "redlegs turtle."

Key identifiers: sculpted shell, orange markings on neck and limbs.

Habitat: Wood turtles live in open woodlands and glades near streams; in and near swamps and bogs; and in wet meadows and old fields. They rarely move more than a few hundred yards from the water (and may enter the water every few days). Wood turtles tend to have linear home ranges that may be a mile in length, although most are smaller.

Feeding habits: These turtles consume plant and animal food obtained both on land and in the water. They eat algae, moss, grass, leaves, flowers (violets are a favorite), mushrooms, berries, insects, earthworms, snails, tadpoles, newborn mice, and carrion. Wood turtles have been seen stomping on the ground with their front feet; the vibrations cause earthworms to surface from their tunnels, whereupon the turtles eat them.

Distinctive behaviors: Wood turtles are among the most terrestrial of turtles. They are active mainly during the day; by night they rest in shallow forms in the soil beneath grass, leaves, and brush, or in the water in shel-tered areas of creeks. During hot weather, they may soak in puddles or streams, or estivate in cool niches beneath vegetation, fallen logs, or other debris. When walking, wood turtles cover the ground more quickly than most other turtles do. They are excellent climbers. Experiments testing food-finding ability in a maze sug-gest a capacity to learn comparable to that of laboratory rats. Wood turtles hibernate during winter, usually in a small stream, in mud or debris on the bottom, sometimes in a muskrat den or burrowed into a stream bank.

Reproduction: Males bite, shove, and ram each other to establish a dominance hierarchy; older, larger indi-viduals may get more opportunities to breed. Mating usually takes place underwater. Although wood turtles may mate at any time during the active (nonhibernating) season, there are two peaks in breeding: one follow-ing emergence in the spring, and the other in autumn. To make her nest, the female finds a sunny area, scoops out a hole with her hind feet, lays four to eight eggs (sometimes as many as eighteen), then tamps down the soil using her feet and the bottom of her shell.

Population trends: Because wood turtles are attractive, intelligent animals that spend a lot of time on land, people encounter them frequently—and all too often capture them, keeping them as pets or selling them (including to collectors in other countries). This practice is illegal in many states, since removing reproducing adults can severely harm local populations. In general, the population of *Clemmys insculpta* is declining because of human depredations and habitat destruction.

When to look: During summer, watch for wood turtles near rivers and streams. You may spot them basking on emergent logs or rocks or foraging in nearby woods or brushy areas.

Similar species: The only other North American turtle that looks like *Clemmys insculpta* is the diamondback terrapin (*Malaclemys terrapin*), which is about the same size and has a similarly sculpted shell. The diamond-back terrapin, however, lives in coastal salt marshes, where the wood turtle is not found.

Western Pond Turtle
(Clemmys marmorata)

Box and Water Turtle Family
(Emydidae)

About the name: "Western" signifies that this turtle lives on the West Coast. "Pond" is a misnomer, since the species occurs mainly in rivers and streams. *Clemmys* is from the Greek *klemmys,* a tortoise; *marmorata* is Latin for "marbled" and describes the pattern of markings on the carapace.

Size at maturity: small to medium. Adults are 5 to 8 inches in length after eight to ten years' growth.

Distribution: The western pond turtle is found west of the crests of the Cascade and Sierra ranges, from Washington to northern Baja California. The largest populations are scattered from southern Oregon to California. Western pond turtles are found in only three sites in Washington, all along the Columbia River. Molecular genetic analyses have confirmed distinct northern and southern subspecies.

Description: The short, broad carapace is widest behind the midsection. The texture is smooth, and the color is olive, dark brown, gray, or black; spots or lines radiate outward from the centers of the scutes. The pale yellow plastron lacks a hinge. The skin is gray, with pale yellow markings on the neck, chin, forelimbs, and tail.

Key identifiers: dark shell, yellow markings on neck, chin, forelimbs.

Habitat: This turtle lives mainly in slow-moving waters of streams and rivers. Western pond turtles are also found occasionally in lakes, sloughs, impoundments, and irrigation ditches. In the preferred stream and river habitat, individuals spend most of their time in pools rather than shallows. The bottom of the waterway may be rocky or muddy, and it generally supports aquatic plants. Some western pond turtles have been found in the brackish waters of estuaries.

Feeding habits: Western pond turtles eat algae and other plants, snails, crayfish, daphnia (water fleas), isopods (scuds), insects (including many caddis fly and dragonfly nymphs), spiders, fish (taken mainly as carrion), and frogs. They practice neustophagia: opening the mouth slightly at the water's surface to filter out food, particularly water fleas, which can be abundant in some habitats. Males eat larger food items than females; they also consume more insects and vertebrates, while the females eat more algae.

Distinctive behaviors: Western pond turtles are active from late May to October in northern California; farther south, they may be out and about during every month. Individuals forage around sunrise and then bask for two or more hours; sometimes they forage again in late afternoon or evening. While feeding, western pond turtles shift from pool to pool within a waterway. They bask on rocks, boulders, logs, stream banks, and tree branches that dip down into the water. Well adapted to living in arid regions, they will dig down into the mud if the waterway starts to dry up. In winter they hibernate underwater, often buried in the mud bottom of a pool in a stream or river.

Reproduction: These turtles have been observed mating in May, June, and late August. Females deposit clutches of two to eleven eggs in sandy or loose soil, usually near the water although sometimes more than a mile away. The peak nesting period is late May to early July. The young generally hatch and leave the nest in late summer or fall, although some overwinter in the nest and dig their way out the following spring.

Population trends: This once-common species is dwindling as people develop and pollute riverine habitat. *Clemmys marmorata* is listed as a federal species of concern; it has been extirpated in British Columbia and Nevada, and is protected in Washington, Oregon, and California. Urban development in southern California has destroyed most populations in that region; populations have also shown significant declines in the northern part of the range, including the Willamette Valley in Oregon.

When to look: These turtles feed in early morning and bask during midmorning. Look for them resting on large rocks, logs, and stream banks.

Similar species: The western pond turtle is California's only native freshwater turtle. In northern Oregon, the western race of the painted turtle (*Chrysemys picta belli*) shares the western pond turtle's range.

Eastern Box Turtle
(Terrapene carolina carolina)

Box and Water Turtle Family
(Emydidae)

About the name: "Box" refers to this turtle's ability to shut itself inside its upper shell and hinged lower shell, as if in a protective box. *Terrapene* is from the Algonquian Indian word for "turtle," and *carolina* refers to the region of the Carolinas, where box turtles are found.

Size at maturity: small to medium. Adults are $4^1/_2$ to $6^1/_2$ inches long; the largest one ever measured had a shell almost 8 inches long.

Distribution: Box turtles inhabit the eastern half of the United States from southern New England to the Florida Keys and from Kansas to Texas. Box turtles live from sea level to above 3,500 feet.

Description: The carapace is high and domed, and the plastron has a conspicuous hinge, which allows for complete closure of the shell. The mahogany brown carapace is decorated with yellow or orange in intricate patterns of lines, bars, spots, or blotches. The shell is fairly smooth, with a low ridge running down the midline of the carapace. Individuals have black to reddish brown skin, often with yellow, red, or orange markings. Females' eyes are brown or yellowish; in 90 percent of males, the eyes are red. Males have longer tails than females, plus a concave carapace.

Key identifiers: high, domelike shell, yellow or orange markings, hinged carapace.

Habitat: Box turtles favor open woodlands. They also use pastures, river bottomlands, marshy meadows, palmetto thickets, and dunes. Although mainly land-dwelling, they swim across ponds and streams when traveling and soak themselves in water during hot weather.

Feeding habits: Juveniles concentrate on animal prey and gradually add more plant matter to their diets as they mature. Box turtles hunt for insects, snails, slugs, earthworms, millipedes, spiders, dragonfly larvae, crayfish—"whatever strikes their fancy, whatever they can catch," writes biologist C. Kenneth Dodd Jr. Plant foods include roots, shoots, buds, leaves, and fruit, particularly wild berries. Box turtles are fond of mushrooms, including some that are poisonous to humans. At times, box turtles feed on vegetables in people's gardens.

Distinctive behaviors: Box turtles are slow and deliberate in their movements. Scientists believe they can distinguish colors in much the same range as humans; box turtles appear to use their vision along with their sense of smell to select ripe fruits and reject unripe ones. Box turtles are active mainly at dawn, during the day, and in the evening. At night they shelter in a "form," a small space worked in among plant stems, grasses, or other vegetation. Box turtles hibernate in winter in soil, heaps of leaves, and other plant debris, sometimes only 2 to 8 inches below the surface. They emerge from February through April, depending on the latitude. Various studies have found home ranges of 2 to 11 acres, and from 82 to 300 yards in diameter.

Reproduction: Females can store sperm in their reproductive systems and produce fertilized eggs up to four years after mating. They favor sandy soil for digging their nests, in which four to six eggs are laid. The eggs are oval, 1 by $1^1/_2$ inches, with a parchmentlike texture to the shell.

Population trends: Box turtles are not as common as they once were. Habitat destruction by humans is an ongoing threat, as intensive farming, housing developments, and suburban sprawl transform the landscape. Many box turtles are killed when trying to cross roads. If small, increasingly isolated populations cannot exchange genes with other populations, box turtles may vanish from areas where they now live. In many states, it is illegal to catch and sell box turtles; unfortunately, some states continue to allow the capturing of turtles to be kept as pets.

When to look: During the day in summer, particularly on clear, warm mornings following rainy nights. Check for box turtles in areas where wild berries are plentiful.

Similar species: The hinged carapace and land-loving habits distinguish this familiar species. Taxonomists recognize four subspecies of box turtle: Eastern, Gulf coast, Florida, and three-toed. The ornate box turtle (*Terrapene ornata*), a closely related western species, is adapted to arid environments.

Diamondback Terrapin
(Malaclemys terrapin)

Box and Water Turtle Family
(Emydidae)

About the name: This turtle is named for the prominent scutes on its carapace, which resemble diamonds; "terrapin" comes from an Algonquian Indian word for turtle. Carl H. Ernst, Roger W. Barbour, and Jeffrey E. Lovich, in *Turtles of the United States and Canada,* state that *Malaclemys* is from the Greek *malakos,* soft, "apparently referring to [the turtles'] soft-bodied molluscan prey," and the Greek *klemmys,* or tortoise.

Size at maturity: small to medium. Adult females are 6 to 9 inches long, while adult males are 4 to 5^1/$_2$ inches in length.

Distribution: The range of the diamondback terrapin wraps around the eastern and southern coasts of North America, from Cape Cod, Massachusetts, to Texas. Taxonomists recognize seven subspecies, or races.

Description: The large scutes of the carapace feature prominent concentric grooves and ridges. The oblong carapace is an overall gray or light brown to black, and the plastron is yellow to green and sometimes black. The skin of the head and neck is generally light colored, spotted and streaked with dark markings. Much individual variation exists in color and marking patterns, both on the skin and the shell. Juveniles sport brighter colors and patterning than adults. The feet of this swimmer are strongly webbed, and the hind feet are large. Females have markedly larger heads than males, plus a well-developed crushing surface on the jaws.

Key identifiers: concentric rings on scutes, mottled or spotted head and legs, brackish or saltwater habitat.

Habitat: Diamondback terrapins live in coastal salt marshes, estuaries, tidal creeks and flats, and the shoreward fringes of barrier islands, often in areas bordered with salt-tolerant *Spartina* grasses.

Feeding habits: Diamondback terrapins eat a range of hard-shelled prey, including salt marsh periwinkles and other mollusks, crabs, and mussels. They also eat carrion, fish, marine worms, and some plant matter.

Distinctive behaviors: Diamondback terrapins are active by day, feeding in salt marshes and basking on the banks of tidal creeks. Well adapted to a brackish habitat, diamondback terrapins are believed to be able to discriminate between waters having different salinities: when an individual's body is charged with salt, it will drink from a source having a low salinity, such as rainwater, including that which collects on its own limbs and shell. The diamondback terrapin has an orbital, or eye, gland that releases tears whose salt concentration is greater than that of seawater. In the northern part of its range, the diamondback terrapin hibernates from November to May; in southern areas, it goes inactive from December to March. Hibernating individually or in small groups, terrapins rest on the bottoms of creeks, buried in creek banks near the high tide line, and beneath undercut banks.

Reproduction: Sometimes these turtles form groups of 75 to 250 individuals during the spring breeding season. Males swim after females for long distances. Most nesting and egg laying happens from April through July. Females nest by day; many dig their nests in barrier-island sand dunes, on the sides facing away from the ocean. Clutch sizes vary from eight to eighteen eggs. In some areas, females lay two clutches per year. The eggs hatch after two to three months, with the temperature in the nest determining the sex of the hatchlings. (Low temperatures yield a predominance of males.) Hatchlings hide by burrowing into wrack at the high tide line.

Population trends: The diamondback terrapin was once the main ingredient in terrapin soup, and those near cities were almost wiped out in the early twentieth century. Since then, most populations south of New York have recovered. This species has lost much of its habitat to coastal development and pollution, which have ruined its feeding areas, killed its shellfish prey, and destroyed its nesting beaches.

When to look: Watch for these turtles during the day. Quietly paddling a canoe along a tidal creek may let you sneak up on basking terrapins.

Similar species: Only a few turtles share the diamondback's brackish habitat. One is the snapping turtle, which is larger and has a long tail with a sawtooth appearance. Another species is the mud turtle; it has a hinged plastron, which the diamondback terrapin lacks.

Common Map Turtle
(Graptemys geographica)

Box and Water Turtle Family
(Emydidae)

About the name: *Graptemys* is from the Greek *graptos,* inscribed (referring to the pattern of markings on the carapace), connected to *emys,* tortoise. The species name *geographica* also refers to the carapace markings, which resemble contour lines on a map.

Size at maturity: medium to large. Males measure 3¹/₂ to 6 inches; females are considerably larger at 7 to 10³/₄ inches.

Distribution: The common map turtle has a discontinuous range that stretches from northwestern Vermont and southern Quebec west through the Great Lakes region to Minnesota; south to New Jersey, Pennsylvania, and Maryland; and south and west to Alabama, Arkansas, and eastern Kansas. Of the nine closely related map turtle species, the common map turtle is the only one that occupies watersheds draining into the Atlantic Ocean.

Description: Think of a topographic map laminated onto a turtle's shell, and you will have an idea of the markings that decorate this reptile. The carapace is oval, rather flat, and bears a low but distinct keel running front to back; the scutes on the back margin of the carapace flare out like saw teeth, particularly in the males. The overall color of the shell is olive green, with an eye-catching array of light and dark stripes and whorls. The plastron is yellow. The head and neck are greenish, with numerous yellow stripes and a roughly triangular yellow mark behind the eye.

Key identifiers: yellow spot behind eyes, maplike markings.

Habitat: Map turtles thrive in large lakes and slow-moving rivers. Basking sites are important habitat features: trees and limbs fallen into the water or partially submerged logs, stumps, and rocks set off a ways from shore and not too close to thick vegetation.

Feeding habits: Common map turtles eat mollusks and crayfish; the females are equipped with large, powerful jaws that let them crush freshwater clams and large snails. Map turtles also consume insects, fish, and a small amount of plant matter. In some habitats, map turtles' feeding habits minimize competition with false map turtles (*Graptemys pseudogeographica*), which eat more insects and vegetation.

Distinctive behaviors: Map turtles are active during daylight, feeding in the morning and the late afternoon and basking during the middle of the day. Gangs of these turtles may bask at the same site; large turtles sometimes shove smaller ones aside or into the water when claiming prime spots. In most of their range, map turtles become active around April and return to hibernation in October or November. Map turtles are fairly cold-resistant, and people have seen them walking sluggishly along beneath ice formed during early cold snaps on northern lakes. These turtles hibernate in deep water on lake or river bottoms. During the part of the year when they are active, individuals of both sexes may shift around within a river habitat, swimming or floating downstream and swimming upstream.

Reproduction: Map turtles breed in both spring and fall. Females nest on land from about May to mid-July, with most clutches laid in the middle of June. Females dig their nest chambers in soft soil or sand, in full sunshine, near lakes and rivers. Typical clutches contain nine to seventeen eggs. Many females nest twice each year, with a typical annual production of twenty-three eggs per female. Environmental temperatures in the nest determine the sex of the embryos.

Population trends: Local populations diminish when water pollution kills off snails or crayfish; development of river- or lakefront properties eliminate nesting habitat; and road traffic kills females when they leave the water to nest.

When to look: During midday, watch for these turtles basking. A spotting scope or binoculars will let you observe individuals interacting at basking sites. If you try to get too close, one of the group will probably see or hear you and quickly dive, causing a cascade of map turtles as the others all go sliding into the water.

Similar species: The other map turtle (*Graptemys*) species have more prominent keels on the carapace, often with noticeable spines.

False Map Turtle
(Graptemys pseudogeographica)

Box and Water Turtle Family
(Emydidae)

About the name: *Graptemys* comes from the Greek *graptos,* inscribed (referring to the pattern of markings on the carapace), linked with *emys,* tortoise; *pseudogeographica* describes a turtle that looks like, but is not the same as, the map turtle, *Graptemys geographica.*

Size at maturity: medium to large. Males are $3^{1}/_{2}$ to $5^{3}/_{4}$ inches long, and females are 6 to $10^{3}/_{4}$ inches.

Distribution: The false map turtle lives in central North America in large streams of the Mississippi and Missouri river drainages. The species' range includes Ohio, Indiana, Illinois, Minnesota, and the Dakotas, and extends south to Mississippi, Louisiana, and Texas.

Description: The false map turtle resembles the common map turtle, but has a distinct keel running along the top of its carapace from neck to tail, including a line of raised projections sometimes called spines. The back rim of the carapace is serrated. The olive to brown carapace has yellow oval or ringlike markings. The skin of the legs, tail, chin, and neck is olive to brown and is decorated with many narrow yellow stripes. The plastron is creamy to yellow. The male false map turtle has very long claws on the front feet.

Key identifiers: yellow spot behind eye, yellow neck stripes that reach the eye, and spines or knobs on the carapace.

Habitat: False map turtles live mainly in large rivers and their backwaters. They also inhabit lakes, ponds, sloughs, bayous, and occasionally marshes. While they prefer slow currents, they also venture into the swift-flowing main channels of rivers.

Feeding habits: False map turtles eat mollusks, insects, carrion, and aquatic plants. In the north, where its range overlaps that of the map turtle, the false map turtle pursues a generalist, omnivorous diet; in southern areas, where map turtles are absent, the false map turtle specializes in eating mollusks, perhaps because it does not need to compete with map turtles for this food resource.

Distinctive behaviors: False map turtles emerge from hibernation around April. After breeding, in May females shift from river channels to areas around islands that offer nesting sites. During summer, both sexes feed in quiet backwaters, and in October or November the turtles return to hibernating in rock piles, soft muddy bottoms, and underground entrances of muskrat lodges and bank burrows. False map turtles bask on muskrat lodges, rocks, logs, sandbars, stumps, and other sites that jut up from the water. False map turtles may use nearly inaccessible basking sites that are shunned by other turtles, including slippery snags angling up steeply from the water's surface.

Reproduction: False map turtles are believed to mate twice a year, in spring and in fall. Not much is known about the details of mating in the wild, but in captivity, the male vibrates his long foreclaws against the female's head. Most females lay their eggs in June. Gravid females linger near nesting beaches, waiting for environmental cues to tell them to leave the water and nest. Clutch sizes range from two to eight eggs, and two and perhaps three clutches are laid yearly. The temperature of the nest determines the sex of the hatchlings and also influences the pattern of yellow markings on the head.

Population trends: Factors that can harm local populations include water pollution, the channelizing and dredging of rivers, siltation, loss of nesting sites, and unlawful shooting.

When to look: Watch for these turtles basking during daylight hours. When frightened, groups of basking false map turtles will all take to the water at once, but they usually return to their basking sites within five or ten minutes.

Similar species: The common map turtle (*Graptemys geographica*) is similar in size and shape, but lacks the spines that stick up from the keel on the false map turtle's carapace.

Red-Eared Slider
(Trachemys scripta elegans)

Box and Water Turtle Family
(Emydidae)

About the name: *Trachemys* is from the Greek *trachys,* rough (referring to the texture of the shell), and *emys,* tortoise. The species name *scripta* is Latin for written and refers to the markings on the carapace, while the subspecies name means "elegant." "Red-eared" describes the red markings behind the eye. Nowhere have I seen a formal explanation for "slider," but these turtles are inveterate baskers that promptly slide off their perches into the water when alarmed, and no doubt that behavior has earned them their common name.

Size at maturity: medium to large. Most adults are 5 to 8 inches, although some exceed 11 inches. Females are larger than males.

Distribution: This turtle is common and abundant in the Midwest and the South. Bred extensively for the pet trade and exported around the world, it has become established in the wild in other parts of North America and in Britain, Europe, Asia, the Middle East, and Australia.

Description: The olive to brown carapace has vertical yellow stripes or bars, which show up most vividly when the shell is wet. The skin, green to olive brown, is also striped with yellow, particularly on the neck and limbs, with a bright red marking behind the eye. Males have elongated, curving foreclaws.

Key identifiers: broad red stripe behind eye, vertical yellow markings on carapace.

Habitat: Sliders live in most freshwater habitats within their range, including lakes, swamps, ponds, and Carolina bays. They prefer still water and a soft bottom with abundant aquatic plants. Some individuals enter the brackish waters of salt marshes.

Feeding habits: Opportunistic omnivores, sliders eat algae, water plants, freshwater sponges, snails, clams, crayfish, spiders, insects, fish, frogs (eggs, tadpoles, and adults), small snakes, and carrion. Young sliders are quite carnivorous. Adults prefer animal foods but tend to eat increasing amounts of vegetation, since it is generally more abundant.

Distinctive behaviors: In the South, sliders may be active during every month of the year. Farther north, they hibernate from around November to March; hibernacula include muskrat burrows and hollow stumps. During the day, sliders patrol for food in shallow waters; while they detect food items mainly by sight, they also use their sense of smell. These turtles bask frequently, both by floating on the surface of sun-warmed water and by crawling onto snags, logs, and rocks. At night, sliders sleep resting on the bottoms of their watery habitat or floating at the surface.

Reproduction: Breeding takes place in spring and fall. Courtship, conducted in the water, is highly stylized: The male stimulates the female by swimming around her and vibrating his long foreclaws against her head near the eyes. Several males may court one female at the same time. Females lay their eggs from April to July, with a peak in May and June. Nests are often dug into levees, on the edges of drainage ditches, and in railroad embankments. About ten eggs are laid; they hatch after two months, in late summer or early fall. The sex of the hatchlings is determined by the temperature inside the nest. Some females lay as many as five clutches in a single year.

Population trends: Some herpetologists judge the red-eared slider the most widespread and least endangered turtle in the world.

When to look: Sliders bask most frequently during midmorning and midafternoon, when they can best be observed through binoculars or a spotting scope. A good way to study them is from inside a car, since they will not become afraid and slide off their perches into the water.

Similar species: Turtles in genera *Trachemys* and *Pseudemys* can be hard to identify, even for biologists and veteran naturalists. Different species can look quite similar to each other, and a number of the species hybridize. Some male sliders are melanistic, turning dark as they age and losing their markings. (At one time, melanistic sliders and nonmelanistic ones were thought to be separate species.) Two other slider subspecies are found in North America: the yellowbelly slider ranges from Virginia to Florida and into Alabama; and the Cumberland slider lives in eastern Tennessee.

River Cooter
(Pseudemys concinna)

Box and Water Turtle Family
(Emydidae)

About the name: *Pseudemys* means that this New World genus resembles but is not the same as the European turtle genus *Emys.* The Latin species name, *concinna,* means neatly or skillfully joined, and probably refers to the smooth shell. "River" denotes this turtle's favorite habitat, and "cooter" comes from *kuta,* an African word for turtle brought to this continent by slaves.

Size at maturity: large. Adults are 9 to 12 inches, with females larger than males.

Distribution: The river cooter ranges from Virginia to Florida and west to eastern Kansas, Oklahoma, and Texas. Taxonomists recognize three to five subspecies or races.

Description: The relatively flat carapace is brown, patterned with yellow to creamy markings in concentric rings. The outermost (marginal) scutes of the carapace have dark, doughnut-shaped marks on their bottom surfaces, visible when the turtle has been turned onto its back. Five yellow stripes adorn the forehead between the eyes, and wide yellow stripes mark the chin and underside of the neck. Adult males have long, straight foreclaws. As they age, many river cooters become quite dark, causing the pattern on the carapace to dim or vanish.

Key identifiers: yellow-striped head and neck, doughnut markings on bottom of carapace rim.

Habitat: River cooters favor rivers having a slow to moderate current, plentiful aquatic plants, and a rocky bottom. They are also found in lakes, ponds, oxbows, swamps, and deep springs. They need basking sites, such as rocks or partly submerged tree trunks.

Feeding habits: Adults eat mainly plants, and they also feed on crayfish, tadpoles, small fish, snails, and insects.

Distinctive behaviors: The activity period for river cooters is roughly April to October; during the cold months, these turtles hibernate in mud on the bottom of a body of water. River cooters bask frequently; one biologist counted forty-seven river cooters sunning themselves on a single log. They often bask in mixed-species groups along with sliders and painted turtles.

Reproduction: River cooters mate in the spring. During courtship the male vibrates his long foreclaws in front of the female's face. Most females nest in late May or June, within 100 feet of the water in sandy or loamy soil. Clutch size ranges from nine to twenty-nine eggs.

Population trends: Although it has dwindled in some areas as a result of human-caused habitat degradation, this species remains relatively abundant in much of its range.

When to look: As with most other river turtles, cooters bask during the middle part of the day and are most easily studied at that time. Extremely wary, they flee from their basking sites if they see or hear a person approaching; a parked automobile makes a good observation post.

Similar species: Turtles in genera *Trachemys* and *Pseudemys* can be quite hard to tell apart. Their life histories are similar, however, and it can be instructive to watch all of the various types and age classes interact while they bask along and on river shores.

Redbelly Turtle
(Pseudemys rubriventris)

Box and Water Turtle Family
(Emydidae)

About the name: *Pseudemys* means that this New World genus resembles but is not the same as the common European pond turtle genus, *Emys;* the Latin *rubriventris* means red-bellied. "Redbelly" refers to the color of the plastron.

Size at maturity: large. Adults are 10 to 12$^{1}/_{2}$ inches long (the record is 15$^{3}/_{4}$ inches), with females slightly larger than males. Throughout much of its range, this will be the biggest basking turtle found.

Distribution: The redbelly turtle lives in the southern half of New Jersey and in southern Pennsylvania and extreme eastern West Virginia, south through Delaware, Maryland, and coastal Virginia to North Carolina. A separate population lives in Plymouth County, Massachusetts, south and east of Boston.

Description: The carapace is brown to black, with vertical red bars and yellow markings. The coloration and marking patterns can vary considerably between individuals. These turtles darken as they age; the markings on the carapace may become dim, but they usually are discernible when the shell is wet. The plastron is reddish orange, with dark smudges or symmetrical markings. The dark olive to black skin is marked with yellow stripes. On the upper jaw, a central notch is flanked by a pair of cusps that look somewhat like fangs. Males possess long, straight foreclaws.

Key identifiers: large size, vertical red markings on carapace.

Habitat: Most redbelly turtles live in fairly deep water, particularly in rivers having a moderate current, and in associated floodplain marshes, oxbows, and ponds. The populations in Massachusetts live in seventeen ponds and one river site. Ideal habitats feature a soft bottom, numerous basking sites, and plenty of plants. In some areas, redbelly turtles venture into brackish waters.

Feeding habits: Young redbelly turtles are omnivorous and consume snails, tadpoles, crayfish, and dead fish, as well as vegetation. Adults develop serrated crushing surfaces on their jaws, which they use to grind up aquatic plants.

Distinctive behaviors: This turtle is active from March into November throughout most of its range. It spends the day feeding or lying in the sun, basking on logs and rocks, often in the company of painted turtles, which are smaller than adult redbelly turtles. When basking sites are limited, painted turtles will shove aside and clamber on top of redbelly turtles, and vice versa.

Reproduction: Redbelly turtles mate in spring. Females lay eggs in June, in clutches of ten to twelve (sometimes as many as thirty-five), in nests excavated in soil near the water. The young hatch after seventy to eighty days.

Population trends: When humans develop shorelines, they destroy nesting and basking sites necessary for this and other turtle species. The Massachusetts redbelly turtles form what is called a disjunct, or relict, population. At present, this population numbers around 300 individuals. It is threatened by genetic isolation, as its members are separated from, and unable to share genetic material with, other redbelly turtles farther south. The small Massachusetts population is listed as endangered by the U.S. Fish and Wildlife Service.

When to look: Midday is a good time to observe redbelly turtles as they bask on rocks, logs, and snags. Use binoculars or a spotting scope to watch interactions when the turtles compete among themselves and with turtles of other species for the basking spots.

Similar species: The river cooter (*Pseudemys concinna*) and cooter (*Pseudemys floridana*) share parts of the redbelly turtle's range. Neither of the cooters have a notch at the tip of the upper jaw, and they are smaller than the redbelly turtle.

Painted Turtle
(Chrysemys picta)

Box and Water Turtle Family
(Emydidae)

About the name: This turtle is named for its colorful shell. *Chrysemys* is from the Greek *chrysos,* gold, and refers to the color of the rim of the carapace; *picta* means "painted."

Size at maturity: small. Adults are 4 to 6 inches long, with females larger than males.

Distribution: The painted turtle has the broadest range of any turtle in North America. It is found from Nova Scotia to Washington State and from southern Canada to Georgia and Texas. Taxonomists recognize four subspecies, or races: eastern, southern, midland, and western. The races intergrade with each other, have overlapping ranges, and share many physical characteristics and behaviors.

Description: The carapace is smooth and noticeably flattened. Scutes are dark olive to black, their leading edges a paler olive color. (This pattern can be seen through binoculars.) The plastron is yellow. Red and yellow stripes adorn the legs, neck, and head, and a pair of bright yellow spots mark the face behind each eye. Males have longer foreclaws than females.

Key identifiers: bright yellow spots on head, large scutes with pale olive edges.

Habitat: Painted turtles live in shallow waters of lakes, ponds, and slow rivers, where the bottom is muddy and grown with vegetation. A key habitat feature is adequate basking sites: half-submerged logs, tree trunks, branches, rocks, muskrat houses, beaver dams, and floating mats of vegetation.

Feeding habits: Painted turtles eat a variety of foods. Animal items include aquatic insects, tadpoles, fish, snails, slugs, small clams, crayfish, and carrion. Plant foods are many and include algae and cattail stems and seeds.

Distinctive behaviors: Painted turtles are well known for basking. They choose spots offering good visibility of the nearby shoreline so they can quickly dive back into the water if danger threatens. Some bask by floating in sunlit water with their limbs extended. In areas where basking sites are few, painted turtles may climb on each others' backs to claim the sunlight. Active for much of the year, painted turtles bury themselves in soft mud underwater to wait out the coldest months. In late winter and early spring in the northern parts of their range, painted turtles have been spotted moving beneath the ice.

Reproduction: Breeding peaks from late April to mid-June. Mating takes place on the lake or river bottom. The male swims around the female in a circle; while facing her, he sweeps the backs of his elongated fore-claws along her head and neck. Females nest mainly in June and July. Most nesting takes place late in the day and often during rain. A typical clutch numbers four to eight eggs (in some cases, as many as twenty are deposited). The eggs hatch after about seventy-five days. In northern areas, the young may overwinter in the nest.

Population trends: In any suitable shallow-water habitat within its range, *Chrysemys picta* is usually the most abundant turtle; in some areas, biologists have estimated populations of more than 200 per acre of aquatic habitat. Habitat destruction and collection for the pet trade and for use as experimental animals has harmed local populations. Popular as pets, painted turtles have been introduced into the wild in many areas.

When to look: Because they bask so frequently, painted turtles are fairly easy to find. Mornings on bright, sunny days in early spring are particularly good times. Use binoculars or a spotting scope to watch social inter-actions and behaviors at crowded basking sites. If you scare the turtles and they dive, wait for a while, as they will usually emerge and reoccupy their basking spots.

Similar species: Of the common basking turtles, the painted is the smallest species. In some northern habi-tats, painted turtles may be the only conspicuous basking turtles.

Chicken Turtle
(Deirochelys reticularia)

Box and Water Turtle Family
(Emydidae)

About the name: *Deirochelys* is from the Greek *deire,* or neck, referring to the extremely long neck of this turtle, combined with *chelys,* tortoise; the Latin word for netted, *reticularia,* describes the reticulate markings on the carapace. The common name recognizes that the flesh of this species, eaten by some people, is good-tasting.

Size at maturity: small to medium. Adults are 4 to 6 inches, with the record carapace length of 10 inches. Females are about one and a half times as large as males.

Distribution: The chicken turtle is found from southeastern Virginia south along the Atlantic coastal plain to southern Florida, and west along the Gulf Coast to Texas and north to Oklahoma, Arkansas, and southeastern Missouri. Taxonomists recognize three races—eastern, Florida, and western—with slightly different markings.

Description: The carapace is tan to olive, overlaid with a network of fine yellow lines; the plastron is yellow. Seen from above, the carapace is oblong and almost pear-shaped in the way that it goes from being narrow at the front to wider at the rear. The plastron is yellow and does not have a hinge. The neck, strongly striped with yellow, is extremely long. The long, narrow head ends in a pointed snout. There is a broad yellow stripe on the front of the forelegs.

Key identifiers: network of fine lines on carapace, extremely long neck with stripey markings.

Habitat: Chicken turtles prefer the still waters of ponds, lakes, marshes, cypress swamps, and ditches, particularly areas with a healthy amount of aquatic vegetation and a soft bottom. They also move far away from the water at times.

Feeding habits: Omnivorous feeders, chicken turtles eat tadpoles, crayfish, and some plants. They forage mainly in the morning, crawling or swimming with the long neck extended. To capture quick-moving animals, particularly small aquatic invertebrates, a chicken turtle will rapidly expand its throat, sucking in water containing its prey.

Distinctive behaviors: Chicken turtles are well adapted to living in ephemeral habitats, such as ponds that dry up in summer. They often wander extensively on land, and individuals of both sexes will migrate from one aquatic habitat to another. In the northern part of the range, chicken turtles spend the winter hibernating in mud and aquatic vegetation; some also hibernate on land. While those in Florida do not hibernate, they remain inactive on cold days. Chicken turtles bask frequently, and like most basking turtles, they are wary and difficult to approach.

Reproduction: When courting a female, the male vibrates his foreclaws against her face. Chicken turtles have a unique nesting pattern. Females lay eggs in late winter to early spring (mid-February to May) and in late fall to early winter (August to November); in Florida, females nest from mid-September through early March. The nests are on land, around 200 feet from the water. Females lay clutches averaging eight or nine eggs. The embryos pause in their development, and a period of chilling is needed before they finish their development. The temperature of the nest influences the sex of the hatchlings. The eggs hatch after three to five months. Some females in Florida lay four clutches per year.

Population trends: Chicken turtles need a combination of aquatic and land habitats for their annual life cycle. Where highways or housing developments cut off travel corridors between these two habitat types, local populations may become extinct. Many chicken turtles are killed on roadways.

When to look: On sunny, warm days, use binoculars or a spotting scope to scan basking turtles from a distance.

Similar species: Because of the variability of color patterns, many of the southern water-dwelling turtles can be hard to identify as to species.

Blanding's Turtle
(Emydoidea blandingii)

Box and Water Turtle Family
(Emydidae)

About the name: "Blanding's" commemorates William Blanding, of Philadelphia, a nineteenth-century physician and naturalist who first described the species. *Emydoidea* means "resembling *Emys*," the genus for European pond turtles, and *blandingii* is another reference to William Blanding.

Size at maturity: medium. Adults are 5 to 7 inches long; the largest specimen ever found had a 10³/₄-inch carapace. The female has a longer plastron and a higher carapace than the male.

Distribution: The species' range centers on the Upper Midwest, from southern Ontario west across Michigan and Wisconsin to Nebraska, and south to Illinois, Indiana, and Ohio. Blanding's turtle is also found in parts of New York, New England, and Nova Scotia.

Description: The carapace is black, marked with tan or yellow streaks and spots that resemble floating duck-weed plants. A good identification mark is the bright yellow chin and throat (the rest of the skin is blue-gray), sometimes visible through binoculars. If you get this turtle in hand, look for the movable hinge on the plastron. (Blanding's turtle is sometimes called the "semi-box turtle," since in some individuals the hinge does not allow for as complete a closure as that achieved by the box turtle.)

Key identifiers: yellow chin and throat, hinged plastron.

Habitat: Blanding's turtles live in marshes, bogs, ponds, lakes, and small streams, where the bottom is covered with decomposed organic matter supporting the growth of aquatic plants. Blanding's turtles avoid thick cattail marshes and ponds or streams with sandy bottoms. At times, Blanding's turtles move about on land.

Feeding habits: Blanding's turtles are largely carnivorous. In the water they eat crayfish (more than 50 percent of the diet in several studies), aquatic insects, fish and fish eggs, tadpoles and frogs, snails, leeches, and plants. On land they consume leaves, grass, berries, slugs, insects, and earthworms.

Distinctive behaviors: This species is notably cold-tolerant. In Minnesota, biologists found that Blanding's turtles became active and remained so at lower temperatures than painted turtles and common snapping turtles in the same habitat. Blanding's turtles are active from April into September. They bask and feed during the day; at night they sleep hidden among plants on the marsh or pond bottom. They bask on muskrat lodges, banks, logs, stumps, driftwood piles, and mats of sedges and cattails. During hot weather they estivate, usually underwater, although sometimes beneath leaf litter on land. In winter Blanding's turtles become dormant, remaining partly buried in the pond bottom.

Reproduction: Blanding's turtles mate from March to July. Biologists have noted eight sequential male behaviors, including chasing the female, climbing onto her carapace, pressing down with the chin ("chinning") on the female's snout, and swaying the head back and forth. Females nest from late May to early July. Most females return to the same general areas where they nested in the past. Some nest close to the home marsh, while others move off a kilometer or farther—a surprisingly long distance for an aquatic turtle. The average clutch is ten to fifteen eggs. Deposited in sandy soil, the eggs hatch after about three months. Hatchlings have a distinctive musky odor, which may let individuals follow trails laid down by other juveniles. Hatchlings spend their first winter at the bottom of a lake, stream, or marsh.

Population trends: As with other turtles, many Blanding's turtles are killed by cars when crossing roads, either traveling to nesting sites or shifting from one aquatic habitat to another. Habitat destruction is also menacing this species. A study on the Illinois River found that populations were harmed by land clearing and the draining of floodplain marshland for agriculture; by the construction of locks and dams; and by sewage pollution.

When to look: Blanding's turtles can be seen in the spring, when basking. They are more active in the morning than at any other time of the day.

Similar species: Like Blanding's turtle, the box turtle (*Terrapene carolina*) has a hinged plastron, but the box turtle lacks the yellow throat and chin of *Emydoidea blandingii*.

Gopher Tortoise
(Gopherus polyphemus)

Gopher Tortoise Family
(Testudinidae)

About the name: "Gopher" signifies this turtle's excellent digging ability. "Tortoise" refers to a group of land-dwelling turtles. *Gopherus* comes from "gopher," and *polyphemus* denotes a strong, cave-dwelling giant of the same name, from Greek mythology.

Size at maturity: medium to large. Adults are 6 to 9^1/$_2$ inches long (the record is 15 inches).

Distribution: Gopher tortoises live in the Deep South, on the coastal plain in extreme southern South Carolina, southern Georgia, much of Florida, southern Alabama, southern Mississippi, and extreme eastern Louisiana.

Description: The carapace is brown or tan, and the plastron is dull yellow; young tortoises show a good deal of orange or yellow on the large scutes of the carapace. The skin is gray on adults and yellow on juveniles. On older adults, the shell is relatively smooth; on younger tortoises, the scutes of the carapace bear conspicuous growth rings. The plastron lacks a hinge and is concave in males and flat in females.

Key identifiers: long, columnar legs and shovel-like forefeet.

Habitat: Well-drained, sandy soils in pine flatwoods, oak hammocks, and scrubland. Fire-adapted trees—sand pine, scrub oak, and longleaf pine—are common in tortoise habitat. Gopher tortoises also live in pastures, old fields, and open, grassy areas near roads. A study in Florida found that the average home range was 7.75 acres.

Feeding habits: Gopher tortoises eat legumes (bean family plants), broadleaf grasses, and plants in the aster (sunflower) family. Despite their defensive spines, prickly pear cactus and stinging nettle are grazed on by gopher tortoises. They also like papaws, saw palmetto berries, blueberries, blackberries, gopher apples, and other fruits.

Distinctive behaviors: The life of a gopher tortoise centers on a tunnel-like burrow that the creature excavates using its shovel-shaped front feet. Burrows are generally 8 to 20 feet long (sometimes as long as 40 feet) and as deep as 10 feet; they are wide enough for a turtle to turn around in. An individual may use three or more burrows during the active season. Although mainly terrestrial, some gopher tortoises will swim across narrow canals and shallow streams.

Reproduction: Courtship and mating take place mainly in the spring. Competition over females can lead to combat between males, who use their gular projections (extensions on the front of the plastron) to ram into one another. In some cases, males get flipped over onto their backs; overturned males will die if they cannot right themselves. Females lay eggs from late April until mid-July, with most nesting taking place in May and June. A female generally digs her nest some distance away from her burrow, in a spot exposed to full sunlight. She lays three to fifteen eggs and covers them with soil. Incubation takes eighty to ninety days in Florida and more than one hundred days in Georgia. Many nests are destroyed by predators, and an individual female gopher tortoise may produce a successful nest only once in every ten years.

Population trends: The gopher tortoise is declining throughout its range. Habitat loss is the most serious threat: Housing development, roads, mining, and conversion of scrublands to citrus culture and forest plantations have destroyed countless acres. Many gopher tortoises are killed on highways. The gopher tortoise is listed as "threatened," "endangered," or a "species of special concern" in all the states where it is found.

When to look: In Florida, gopher tortoises are active year-round; during cold snaps, tortoises stay mainly in their burrows and emerge to feed on warm days. In one study, biologists found tortoises wandering about from 10 AM to 2 PM; at other times, they were underground.

Similar species: The eastern box turtle is occasionally misidentified as a young gopher tortoise, but the gopher tortoise lacks the box turtle's hinged plastron.

Desert Tortoise
(Gopherus agassizii)

Gopher Tortoise Family
(Testudinidae)

About the name: "Desert" describes the environment where this turtle is found. "Tortoise" refers to a group of land-dwelling turtles. *Gopherus* derives from "gopher," the burrowing rodent (many tortoises in this genus are accomplished burrowers), and *agassizii* honors the nineteenth-century naturalist Jean Louis R. Agassiz.

Size at maturity: large. Adults are 9 to 15 inches long and weigh 8 to 15 pounds; males are larger than females.

Distribution: Desert tortoises live in the Mojave and Sonoran Deserts of southeastern California, southern Nevada, Arizona, southwestern Utah, and northern Mexico. The species' range reaches an elevation of at least 3,500 feet.

Description: The carapace is oblong and domed, highest slightly back of the middle; its surface is rough and ridged, with prominent raised scutes. The scutes are black to tan, often with brown or orangish centers, particularly on younger individuals. The legs are brown, and the head is tan. The sturdy, columnar legs end in large hind feet and forefeet that are shaped like shovels. The toes are not webbed and are tipped with substantial black claws. Males have thicker tails than females and are equipped with a gular projection, a forward-facing extension of the plastron, just below the neck.

Key identifiers: large size, rough shell, long columnar legs.

Habitat: Desert tortoises in California, Nevada, Utah, and northern Arizona occupy valleys, flats, alluvial fans, and washes, among Joshua trees and Mojave yuccas, creosote bush, and saltbush scrub. Populations in the Sonoran Desert of Arizona live on steep, rocky hillsides, many of which are cloaked with paloverde and saguaro cactus. In all areas where they are found, desert tortoises require soils into which they can burrow, as well as a dependable supply of forage plants.

Feeding habits: Desert tortoises are mainly herbivores, eating a variety of grasses, cacti, and annual and perennial plants. They particularly like spring flowers. They consume the succulent pads and buds of cacti, an important source of water during dry spells.

Distinctive behaviors: Desert tortoises spend most of their lives underground, in burrows that they dig themselves, using their powerful forelimbs. A burrow may be only a foot deep, or it may extend 3 to 10 feet into a hillside or the side of a wash. In the spring, desert tortoises may be out and about all day long. As summer's heat increases, the tortoises leave their burrows around sunrise and forage for a while, rest in their burrows during midday, then feed again in late afternoon or evening. During rainstorms, they drink their fill; individuals may dig small basins in the dirt to hold water, making it easier to drink. Desert tortoises are good climbers, able to ascend steep and rocky slopes. They hibernate in individual burrows, or in communal dens; in the latter (often enlarged ground squirrel burrows), up to twenty-three individual tortoises have been found. The tortoises leave their hibernation from February to April and remain active until October or November.

Reproduction: Courtship and mating take place from spring into fall. A male will trail a female, bobbing his head. Once she stops, the male will begin biting her on the snout, forelegs, and shell. One mating may fertilize several clutches of eggs. Females lay their eggs from May through July. One to twelve eggs are deposited per clutch, in holes dug in the earth at the mouths of burrows, inside the burrows, or elsewhere. The eggs, about the size and shape of Ping-Pong balls, hatch in 70 to 120 days. Some females nest two or three times in a year.

Population trends: In many areas, desert tortoise numbers are falling. Factors include people illegally collecting them as pets; loss of habitat from road construction, mining, and military activities; the use of off-road vehicles in desert areas (the machines kill tortoises directly and destroy their food plants); and diseases introduced to wild populations when people release sick captive tortoises back into the wild.

When to look: In the Mojave and Colorado Deserts, tortoises are most active in late winter and spring (late March through May), from midmorning to midafternoon. In the Sonoran Desert, they may be more active in summer and early fall.

Similar species: With their rough shells, desert tortoises are distinctive. The most similar-appearing species is probably the wood turtle (*Clemmys insculpta*), which is not found in the U.S. Southwest.

Smooth Softshell
(Apalone mutica)

Softshell Turtle Family
(Trionychidae)

About the name: "Smooth" describes the surface texture of the carapace. *Apalone* is derived from the Greek *apo,* separate, and the Anglo-Saxon "alone," and refers to an isolated population of softshell turtles along the Hudson River; *mutica* is Latin for "curtailed" or "cut off" and refers to the absence of spines on the carapace's leading edge.

Size at maturity: medium to large. Males are 4^1/$_2$ to 7 inches long. Females are 6^1/$_2$ to 14 inches–half again as large as the males.

Distribution: Smooth softshells inhabit the central region of North America, including the Ohio, Mississippi, and Missouri river drainages–essentially from Ohio to Wisconsin, Minnesota, and the Dakotas, and south to the Florida Panhandle, the Gulf Coast states, and Texas.

Description: The carapace is round, flat, and flexible, with a smooth, leathery surface. The shell is olive to orangish brown, overlaid with darker dots, short lines, and blotches. The skeletal bones may be visible through the white or gray plastron. The nose is long and the nostrils round; the nostrils lack the small interior ridges possessed by the spiny softshell. The strongly webbed feet have three claws.

Key identifiers: smooth leathery carapace, long tapering snout.

Habitat: Smooth softshells live in large rivers, creeks, and streams. Although some individuals reside in lakes and ponds, smooth softshells are less likely to inhabit still waters than are spiny softshells. Smooth softshells inhabit waterways with sandy bottoms and some rocks and aquatic plants. Hatchlings favor warm shallows along the complex shores of sandbars.

Feeding habits: Softshell turtles concentrate on insects, mostly aquatic types and mainly in the larval stages, such as dragonfly naiads, mayfly nymphs, caddis flies, and bugs. They also eat worms, snails, clams, crayfish, spiders, fish (both small fish, taken alive, and larger fish, eaten as carrion), frogs and tadpoles, mud puppies, and the occasional young bird or small mammal. Softshells eat a minor amount of algae and other vegetable items, such as seeds, nuts, and berries found along the water's edge. They have extremely sharp jaws for slicing apart prey.

Distinctive behaviors: Softshell turtles are strong, fast swimmers that can chase down small fish underwater. They feed using a peer-and-probe technique (thrusting their heads in among underwater vegetation), dig themselves into the sand to wait and ambush their prey, and gulp in water containing small animals. Active by day, they may bask on beaches within a few feet of the water. Because their leathery skin loses moisture quickly, these turtles do not spend much time on land. Females have large home ranges, moving up and down rivers; males' home areas are smaller. Softshells hibernate during the colder months, burying themselves in the sandy bottoms of waterways.

Reproduction: Softshells mate after emerging from hibernation in the spring. Males hunt for receptive females, swimming through the habitat and checking out basking individuals. An unreceptive basking female may bite an inquisitive suitor and inflict a bleeding wound on the carapace. Mating takes place in deep water. The females dig nests and lay eggs in higher zones of exposed sandbars; where suitable sites are limited, nests may be within a few feet of one another and may even have connected egg chambers. If floods cover sandbars for more than a few days, the eggs may not hatch. Typical clutches contain fourteen to twenty-two eggs. Many females lay two clutches yearly. After about two months, the young hatch in August or September. The temperature of the nest chamber does not determine the sex of hatchlings (as it does in many other turtle species).

Population trends: Channelizing and damming rivers and developing their shorelines destroy nesting and feeding habitats and have eliminated some local populations. In the Illinois River, smooth softshell numbers fell after erosion from the surrounding landscape silted over nesting beaches. Draining wetlands and sewage pollution also harm softshells.

When to look: Slowly canoeing along free-running streams and rivers may afford a glimpse of these shy, wary turtles as they bask on sandbars and on rocks and logs.

Similar species: The spiny softshell (*Apalone spinifera*) looks similar but has spines or knobs on the front edge of the carapace.

Spiny Softshell
(Apalone spinifera)

Softshell Turtle Family
(Trionychidae)

About the name: "Spiny" describes the surface texture of the carapace. *Apalone* is derived from the Greek *apo,* "separate," plus the Anglo-Saxon "alone," and refers to an isolated population of softshell turtles along the Hudson River; *spinifera* is Latin for "spiny" and also refers to the rough carapace.

Size at maturity: medium to large. Males are 5 to 9 inches long; females are 7 to 17 inches, or approximately one and a half times as large as the males.

Distribution: Spiny softshells range from western Pennsylvania and New York to South Dakota, Wyoming, and Colorado, and south to Florida, the Gulf Coast states, Texas, and Mexico. Outlying populations inhabit rivers in Montana, the Desert Southwest, and California.

Description: The carapace is round, flat, and flexible. Its surface is sandpapery, and small conical spines project from the leading edge. The carapace is colored olive to tan, overlaid with dark spots. The plastron is white or yellow. The long snout ends in round nostrils, each of which has a small interior ridge. The webbed feet have three claws.

Key identifiers: leathery carapace with spines at front, long tapering snout.

Habitat: Spiny softshells live mainly in rivers, creeks, streams, and canals. They also reside in bayous, lakes, river oxbows, and ponds, inhabiting such still waters to a greater extent than smooth softshells. Underwater brush, sunken trees, and other debris make a habitat more attractive to spiny softshells.

Feeding habits: Largely carnivorous, these turtle eat insects, crayfish, fish (small ones caught and swallowed alive, and larger fish consumed as carrion), plus a small amount of plant matter.

Distinctive behaviors: In the North, spiny softshells are active from April or May through September or October; in the South, they may be out and about in all months. Spiny softshells sleep at night, buried in mud or sand underwater or tucked in among the branches of submerged trees. When underwater, these turtles get oxygen by pumping water into and out of their throats an average of sixteen times per minute; the turtles also get olfactory cues from the water thus processed. Spiny softshells can exchange gases through their skin (including the leathery carapace) both when underwater and on land. A spiny softshell can change its color over the course of a few months, darkening or lightening its skin and markings to match the bottom shading of its habitat. The spiny softshell has a nastier disposition than the smooth softshell; when captured, this turtle bites and scratches vigorously in self-defense.

Reproduction: Spiny softshells mate in April or May; June and July are the main months for nesting. Females dig their nests in areas of full sunlight near the water, often in sandbars and gravel bars, although some females move inland as far as 100 yards. Typical clutches contain twelve to eighteen eggs, which hatch about three months after they were laid. Hatchlings emerge from late August to October. Some juveniles exit their shells, then hibernate in the nest over winter and dig their way to daylight in the spring.

Population trends: When people channelize and dam rivers, and develop their shorelines, they ruin the nesting and feeding habitats necessary for spiny softshells. Other practices that may harm softshell turtles include draining wetlands, polluting waterways with sewage, and building canal locks on free-running waterways.

When to look: Quietly floating in a canoe down a stream or river may earn you an encounter with one of these intriguing turtles. They are extremely wary: Basking on shore, they usually point their heads toward the water so that they can regain that safe environment in a split second.

Similar species: The smooth softshell (*Apalone mutica*) looks similar, but it lacks the spines or knobs found on the leading edge of the spiny softshell's carapace. Also, the smooth softshell does not have the small interior ridges that mark the nostrils of the spiny softshell.

6

Observing Turtles

To improve your chances of spotting and observing turtles in the wild, learn about their habitats and their habits: where they live, and how and when they use different features of the environment. You should also understand how they employ their senses to protect themselves from potential predators.

One of the best ways to spot aquatic and semiaquatic turtles is to locate them basking: lying out in the direct sunlight. During the times of the year when they are not hibernating—from around April through October in much of North America—turtles periodically bask on the edges of water bodies, reposing on rocks, mud and gravel banks, sandbars, fallen trees, snags, floating debris, sedge tussocks, and beaver dams and lodges. Turtles often bask in the morning. They do not bask when it's cold and rainy, but they will sometimes bask on warm overcast days or during a warm rain. Early spring is a particularly good time to find them, recently emerged from hibernation and out soaking up the invigorating rays of the sun.

Turtles have good eyesight and keen hearing, so if you can avoid alerting them by sudden movements and loud noises, you will have a much better chance of watching them for extended periods. Try making your observations from a distance. A pair of good-quality binoculars are a must; in some situations, a tripod-mounted spotting scope can be very effective in letting you identify different species. (Take along a field guide; see the "Resources" section at the back of this book for recommendations.) Some naturalists park their automobiles near suitable habitats and watch out the window, which does not generally alarm turtles. Train your eyes to recognize the small dark bumps of turtle heads dimpling the water, and to pick up part of an animal: a portion of a carapace partly obscured by vegetation, for example. Look out for movement and then unobtrusively shift your binoculars to it. Try stationing yourself near a decaying fish carcass, which may attract carrion-feeding turtles. While walking, if you happen to scare turtles off a basking perch, find a good spot—somewhat hidden but affording a view of the basking area—and sit down quietly and wait for five or ten minutes. Usually at least some of the turtles will get back out of the water and reclaim their basking sites.

Watch how individuals interact when basking. Some turtles pay no attention to other turtles in the vicinity. Others direct open-mouth gestures toward their neighbors; the second turtle may turn away from the aggressive one, change spots at the basking site, or respond by opening its own mouth in a threatening manner. At times, turtles bite one another on the shell or limbs, but this is not a common behavior. Look for turtles stacked one on top of another. You may see a lower turtle try to shake off the one on the top, particularly if the uppermost turtle is large. When you find turtles stacked up this way, it probably signals a dearth of good basking sites in the habitat.

After turtles warm themselves up by basking, they will usually begin foraging for food. Many nature centers and wildlife refuges have lookout towers or observation decks built on the edges of water bodies or extending out into wetlands. From such outposts you may be able to watch turtles feeding in shallows; look closely in areas where underwater vegetation emerges from the water. Bridges, road embankments, and hills that elevate you above the water can also be excellent lookout posts. Turtles are much easier to spot and observe when you are above them; a position on high will better reveal what they are doing, plus cut down on any glare off the water. Slowly paddling a canoe or a kayak through a watery habitat is an excellent way to sneak up on aquatic and semiaquatic turtles. Paddle quietly through shallow areas. In the spring, before summer's rank vegetation has accumulated, you may spot snapping turtles and other species basking or feeding in the water; the top portions of snappers' shells often stick up like muddy mounds. Make your way slowly up the inlet streams that meander into lakes, ponds, and reservoirs. Or choose a slow river or creek and let the current carry your craft downstream, steering quietly and slowing yourself down using your paddle. As you round a bend, you may come upon a shoal of basking turtles—expect them to spot you at some point and go cascading noisily into the water.

Some turtles—snapping turtles, for instance—are active at dusk, during the night, and at dawn. In the dark, use a flashlight or headlamp to look for them along the margins of lakes or ponds, as you walk quietly on a trail near the water's edge or search from a boat. It's easier to see submerged turtles when there is no breeze and the water is still. Musk and mud turtles are strongly nocturnal and sometimes can be spotted in shallows with the aid of a handheld light. Just after daybreak can be a productive time to see turtles as well as other wildlife. In the early morning, turtles may rise to the surface of watery habitats and extend their heads and necks to fill their lungs with air.

During the spring breeding season, male snapping turtles may call attention to themselves when they engage in dominance struggles by wrestling noisily in the shallows of lakes and ponds. Other turtles will be especially active at this time of the year as well, basking and looking for mates. In early summer— particularly from mid-June to late June—hike along on a shoreline, or on a sandy or dirt road or a railroad track leading through a marshy area, and you may encounter a female snapping turtle or perhaps a Blanding's turtle looking for a place to nest. (Many other North American turtles nest at night, although you may also encounter them early in the morning or in the evening.) If you spot a turtle before it has nested, follow it patiently and remain far enough away that you do not alarm it, and you may be rewarded by seeing it dig its nest and lay eggs. You have to be very lucky to find a nesting turtle. But even if you don't spot an actual turtle, a hike at this time of year in a known nesting area may reveal turtle nests that predators have broken into to get at the eggs.

Never harass any turtle. Although a snapping turtle may seem slow and awkward on land, it can turn quickly, lunge forward, and shoot out its long neck and massive head to bite at its tormentor—or at a person who simply gets too close. Some people like to grab hold of a snapping turtle's tail and hoist the animal up; this practice can damage the turtle's spinal column, and it may also result in a severely bitten hand or leg. Many other turtles also react aggressively if they perceive you to be a predator. In most cases, it's best just to watch and let them go about their business. A good way to locate a box turtle or a wood turtle is to spend time hiking on trails through woods near streams and ponds. These terrestrial turtles are often out and about on mornings following summer rain-storms. During hot, dry weather, try looking in shallow pools, streams, and puddles, where the turtles wallow to get cool. (Another interesting way to find terrestrial turtles is to use a dog: Hunting breeds in particular are almost always interested in the scents that turtles emit. Be sure to keep any dog under control, as canines have been known to attack and injure or kill turtles.)

If you find a turtle, retire quietly and keep an eye on the reptile; you may be able to see it finding food and eating. Should you opt for a closer look, the smaller land turtles will usually react timidly, withdrawing the head and limbs into the shell. You can pick them up and study the physical characteristics of skin, scales, legs, feet, and claws; of head and mouth and eyes. Note the subtle but distinctive markings on the shell; try counting annual growth rings on the scutes of the plastron, if these are discernible. Finally, place the turtle back on the ground and retreat. If you wait patiently (very patiently, in some cases), you may then be able to observe it get back to whatever it was doing.

Nature centers, state and national parks, and wildlife refuges sometimes put on programs about turtles, and interpreters lead walks or boat excursions through turtle habitats. For a more intense educational experience, try contacting a local college or university. At times, research biologists or graduate students may allow volunteers to help them trap, mark, and monitor turtles. Some states are in the process of developing and updating atlases of the different species of reptiles and amphibians found within their boundaries. Contact your state wildlife department and inquire about herpetologists working in your area—both professionals and committed amateurs. These enthusiasts are almost always willing to share their knowledge of prime turtle habitats and viewing opportunities and will probably welcome your help in searching for turtles.

7

How You Can Help

In a foreword to the book *Turtle Conservation*, Florida wildlife ecologist Nat Frazer laments "a deep ignorance on the part of the general public" regarding turtles. One of the first things people learn about these creatures, he writes, is the simplistic notion that "the turtle carries his house on his back wherever he goes." Frazer continues: "Surely, a public that thinks turtles are carrying their comfortable homes around with them . . . will not be concerned that we could possibly deprive turtles of suitable habitats in which to live."

Second, Frazer cites a lack of understanding of turtles' life strategies, in which high rates of mortality in eggs and hatchlings are balanced by low death rates among adults and long reproductive lives once turtles reach sexual maturity. "Unfortunately for turtles," he notes, "we have reversed this selective regime in many places, continuously depleting the eggs and young while increasing the mortality rates of adult turtles through habitat destruction and exploitation." Make no mistake about it: Turtles are in serious trouble. In fact, many turtles that people see today—particularly in places like the highly developed Northeast and Southeast, and in southern California—are members of what ecologists call "living-dead" populations. Explains Michael Klemens, a herpetologist at the American Museum of Natural History and the editor of *Turtle Conservation*: "These populations are increasingly composed of aged adults with limited reproductive capability" owing to high mortality rates caused by human activities and habitat loss. Writes Klemens, "Without the benefit of recruitment of young turtles into these populations, either through reproduction or immigration (when possible), over the next decades these populations will continue to decline. Turtles will become increasingly rare and [may] even disappear in many areas where they are now considered secure."

The first thing that a member of the general public can and should do to help save turtles is to educate himself or herself regarding these reptiles' life histories and requirements. If their habitats are not protected, and if adults continue to be removed from the wild (whether by people who decide it would be fun to have a turtle as a pet, or through the deaths of turtles from our automobiles, farming activities, and other practices), turtle numbers will keep falling, and we will lose many more local populations and perhaps even some species.

When you have learned about turtles, you can make better decisions regarding your own behaviors and lifestyle—decisions that can safeguard turtles and many other small and unobtrusive animals with whom they, and we, share the planet. You can pass on your knowledge to young people who will be making important societal decisions in years to come. You can make your peers aware of the ways in which human activities and constructions—highways, dams, housing projects, mechanized forestry, and certain agricultural practices—have a cumulative impact on turtles. If enough people understand the threats to turtles, as well as their particular biological needs, perhaps we can summon the will to halt the trend of dwindling populations—and even reverse it.

Improving Our Understanding of Turtles

Volunteer to serve on a school board and make sure that accurate scientific facts about turtles and other reptiles are taught to students, particularly in elementary and middle schools. Educational programs can foster regional pride in the presence of rare or endangered species; often, local people will get involved with conservation when it is a "grassroots" effort rather than a program mandated by a state or federal agency. Join a herpetology organization (states, regions, and cities have them; see the "Resources" section). These nonprofit groups can make suggestions concerning educational programs and can supply educational materials; they may also put you in touch with scientists and committed amateur herpetologists who will make presentations to school children, wildlife interest clubs, and planning groups. Educate yourself about environmental issues affecting turtles, both locally and nationally, including habitat fragmentation and loss, effects of exotic animals and plants, problems caused by capturing and removing turtles from the wild, pollution, and the draining and destruction of wetlands.

Preventing Habitat Loss

Often a person will look at ongoing habitat loss (one more car dealership along a busy suburban highway, yet another housing development on what was once farmland), shrug, and figure he or she cannot do anything to prevent such environmental deterioration. In fact, there are things that each of us can do to slow this attrition. For example, wooded swamps, ephemeral or seasonal wetlands, and wet meadows are extremely important microhabitats necessary for the survival of many North American turtles. Often people destroy these wetlands, even though such practices are illegal. Developers clandestinely fill them in, and individuals use them as dumps. Report such violations to local, state, and federal wildlife authorities. Often violators will be fined and, more important, be forced to restore these habitats to the way they once were.

Good planning can go a long way toward protecting the environment for turtles. Runoff from roads and houses—frequently polluted with oil and salt from the roads, and with fertilizers and pesticides from lawns—is often channeled or piped into wetlands, severely degrading them. Planners can require developers to create retaining ponds where polluted water can be treated or isolated from natural habitats. High curbs along roads often act as drift fences, stopping turtles, salamanders, and snakes that are trying to cross the roads; these creatures then proceed along the bases of the curbs until they fall into a stormwater drain and drown. Planning commissions can ask developers to hire wildlife consultants to work out ways of eliminating or minimizing these death traps.

Human Recreation

The use of off-road vehicles is increasing in many parts of the United States. Dune buggies, motorcycles, four-wheel-drive vehicles, and ATVs (all-terrain vehicles) have killed many desert tortoises in the American Southwest. Elsewhere, these machines kill other terrestrial turtles; they also compact soils and destroy native vegetation, leading to erosion that can severely damage a habitat. If you use an off-road vehicle, do so gently and carefully and only on trails set aside for such activities. Consider hiking rather than off-roading, and urge friends and family members to do the same.

Even passive recreation can affect turtles. Two wood turtle populations in Connecticut were stable until their areas were opened to hiking and fishing; both populations were gone within a decade. Scientists determined that the turtles vanished because people collected them as pets; they were killed on roads providing access to the recreational areas; and individual turtles were harmed and disturbed by thoughtless humans and dogs. Also, the researchers found evidence that the littering of food attracted raccoons, which are known turtle predators. When you go hiking, keep your dog under control. And never remove a turtle from the wild.

It is an unfortunate truth that people sometimes use turtles for target practice, particularly ones basking on the edges of water bodies. Such illegal and dangerous activities should cease. They should be reported to the authorities at once.

Turtles and Highways

A tremendous number of turtles are killed each year when crossing highways. Some of these individuals are shifting from one part of their habitat to another—for instance, a turtle leaving a pond that is drying out in midsummer and heading toward a site where it can estivate on land. Many others are adult females trying to reach ground suitable for digging a nest and laying eggs. A simple thing you can do to help a turtle in such a situation is to make sure the animal gets across the road. Slow down, turn on your vehicle's flashers, and find a safe place to pull over. The presence of your vehicle, parked on the berm, may alert other drivers that something out of the ordinary is taking place, and they will slow down and avoid hitting the turtle, which will then make it across the road on its own. If you decide to speed up the process, keep your own well-being firmly in mind. Be sure that you won't get hit by a passing car. When it's completely safe to do so, pick the turtle up and carry it to the side of the road toward which it was traveling. When picking up a turtle, always remember to keep its head (and jaws) pointed away from your body. Use two hands, one on each side of the shell, roughly in the middle. Hold the reptile so that if it voids the contents of its cloaca (a not-uncommon defensive behavior), what comes out will end up on the ground and not on your clothing. Never pick up a snapping turtle or a softshell turtle, as these active, aggressive beasts can inflict a serious bite. And, while you are doing the turtle a favor, enjoy the beauty, seen close-up, of a perfectly evolved wild creature—and consider as well the poignancy of its inability to adapt to the changes humans have wrought on the land.

There are other, more-forward-looking ways of helping turtles get across roads. When living in Pennsylvania, I served on a township planning commission. In that capacity, I volunteered to represent our township on a citizens' advisory committee working with the state department of transportation in laying out a proposed interstate highway. During discussions about where to site the road (which, I am happy to say, was not built—or at least has not yet been built), I raised the issue of the number of reptiles and amphibians that would be killed by a new highway cutting through a natural landscape. I strongly advocated that the road be built on top of an existing highway, so that less land would be destroyed. I also requested that the transportation agency hire biologists to locate wildlife corridors (areas through which animals naturally move when traveling through their habitat) and plan to incorporate wildlife underpasses into the road design at those critical points. I doubt that the transportation agency would willingly have gone to the expense of identifying corridors and constructing safe crossings, but I determined to work hard to make them see the importance of fitting the highway into the environment and minimizing its effects on turtles and other animals.

As conservationists and wildlife enthusiasts, we must take a personal responsibility for safeguarding our natural heritage. An excellent way to do this is by volunteering to serve on a local or a regional planning commission. It's also important to attend planning meetings and, in an informed and polite manner, express to planners and officials the particular needs of turtles and other creatures. You can also provide written comments during the public comment phase of proposed projects, and ask questions of and demand help from your elected representatives. Finally, you can vote your conservation convictions in local and national elections.

Atlases and Censusing

Want to contribute to our understanding of and knowledge about turtles, and the presence and abundance of different species? Volunteer for one of the statewide atlas projects aimed at identifying and confirming the ranges of reptiles and amphibians. This will introduce you to professional and amateur herpetologists with knowledge of your region's turtles and their life histories and habits. Many states have posted their atlas data online; studying the maps will show you where different species are found in your state. The data are also used by wildlife biologists seeking to monitor changes in populations. And they help inform land-use planning decisions: One of the goals of an atlas project is to document the distribution and abundance of rare and endangered species.

"Headstarting" Turtles

"Headstarting" is the process of rearing juvenile turtles to a certain size before releasing them into the wild. This practice has been applied to sea turtles and to several species of land turtles, including redbelly turtles in Massachusetts, western pond turtles in Washington State, Blanding's turtles in Nova Scotia, and wood turtles in New York. Generally, biologists locate turtle nests and bring the eggs into the lab for hatching and rearing of young. Headstarting programs can increase the visibility of turtles in the public eye, making people more aware of the problems faced by turtles today. Headstarting programs are often sponsored by zoos and academic institutions, which may welcome volunteer help for both laboratory and field tasks. (The benefits of headstarting have been debated by herpetologists, who point out that if other problems are not solved, such as habitat loss, raising and releasing juveniles may not help local populations in the long run. Also, young turtles may need to move, on their own, from nest sites to the water in order to begin learning their way around the habitat.)

Turtles as Pets

The popular (and excellent) *Reptiles and Amphibians of Eastern and Central North America,* in the Peterson Field Guide series, was first published in 1958. The most recent edition, brought out in 1998, contains—perhaps as a holdover from the 1958 edition—a debatable line: "There is no harm in keeping amphibians and reptiles as pets, at least those that are not rare or endangered in nature." The book also includes chapters on "Making and Transporting the Catch" and

"Care in Captivity." In the half century that has passed since the field guide was first published, many reptile and amphibian populations have fallen radically on this continent. It is true that some turtles remain common and abundant (the red-eared slider, for example), but many other species, including box turtles, wood turtles, bog turtles, and all of the tortoises, are dwindling dangerously in some areas. Today, the best policy is to study turtles in the field and to resist capturing them and keeping them as pets.

There are several reasons that this restraint has become necessary. Taking even one adult out of a breeding population can have a dire outcome—you may never see the effect directly, but the loss of a single individual's reproductive potential could ultimately cause a small population to vanish in a local area: a stream valley, for instance, or a woodland bounded by roads. The more small populations that wink out, the harder it is for a species to exchange genetic material across its range and react to environmental change—and therefore the harder it is for that species to survive. Another important issue is disease: Writes Klemens in *Turtle Conservation,* "Outbreaks of disease in wild turtle populations are increasing, and some outbreaks have been attributed to animals that have been infected in captivity and released into the wild," where they then infect free-ranging turtles.

If you decide to keep a turtle as a pet, do not get it from the wild (which is often illegal for certain species in many areas). Be sure you obtain it from a breeder who has actually produced the animal in a closed operation, out of domesticated stock that has not been collected from the wild any time recently. And if you own a turtle, never release it into nature. You may be able to find an animal rehabilitator who will accept an unwanted turtle, and there is a website that provides adoption and placement for reptiles and amphibians (see "Resources").

Global Warming

Polls reveal that more and more Americans understand that global warming (also called climate change) is actual and ongoing and represents a threat to life on earth as we know it. If temperatures rise too high, they're likely to have a severe effect on turtle reproduction. Scientists have recently discovered that the temperatures at which turtle eggs are incubated determines the sex of the hatchlings (see the section on "TSD and GSD" in chapter 4, "Reproduction"). If high temperatures cause all the nests in a given area to yield only males or females, local populations may be wiped out. Let's all do what we can to conserve, drive less, consume fewer resources, and treat the planet—and its less adaptable denizens, such as turtles—with greater care.

RESOURCES

Books about Turtles

Diamonds in the Marsh: A Natural History of the Diamondback Terrapin, by Barbara Brennessel. Lebanon, NH: University Press of New England, 2006. A Massachusetts biologist takes a close look at the diamondback terrapin.

The Ecology, Exploitation, and Conservation of River Turtles, by Don Moll and Edward O. Moll. New York, NY: Oxford University Press, 2004. A discussion of river turtles worldwide.

Encyclopedia of Turtles, by Peter Pritchard. Neptune City, NJ: TFH Publications, 1979. A encyclopedic treatment of turtle biology written by a leading herpetologist.

A Guide to Amphibians and Reptiles, by Thomas Tyning. Boston, MA: Little, Brown, 1990. Written by a master naturalist, this highly readable book provides information on the biology and behaviors of North American frogs, salamanders, lizards, crocodilians, snakes, and turtles.

Herpetology: An Introductory Biology of Amphibians and Reptiles, by George R. Zug. San Diego, CA: Academic Press, 1993. A college-level text about amphibians and reptiles, with a section on turtles.

The Life History and Ecology of the Slider Turtle, by J. Whitfield Gibbons. New York, NY: HarperCollins, 2000. This volume is based on more than twenty years of studying sliders in South Carolina.

North American Box Turtles, by C. Kenneth Dodd Jr. Norman, OK: University of Oklahoma Press, 2001. A summary of the scientific literature about box turtles and a description of their biology and natural history.

The Reptiles, by Archie Carr. New York, NY: Time-Life International, 1964. This older book remains a readable and informative overview of reptiles in general.

Turtle Conservation, by Michael Klemens, ed. Washington, DC: Smithsonian Institution Press, 2000. A survey of the problems facing North American turtles and efforts to conserve turtles.

Turtles of the United States and Canada, by Carl H. Ernst, Roger W. Barbour, and Jeffrey E. Lovich. Washington, DC: Smithsonian Institution Press, 1994. A rigorous and detailed description of all the turtle species found in North America.

Turtles: Perspectives and Research, by Marion Harless and Henry Morlock. New York, NY: John Wiley & Sons, 1979. Although almost thirty years old, this compilation of scientific papers covers many aspects of turtle biology and contains much useful information.

Turtles, Tortoises, and Terrapins: Survivors in Armor, by Ronald Orenstein. Buffalo, NY: Firefly Books, 2001. Written by a Canadian zoologist, this volume covers turtles worldwide and includes up-to-date information on the natural history of many North American species. The numerous color photographs are superb.

Turtles, Tortoises, and Terrapins, by Fritz Jürgen Obst. New York, NY: St. Martin's Press, 1986. This general account by a German herpetologist describes turtle evolution and adaptations and turtles around the world.

Year of the Turtle: A Natural History, by David M. Carroll. New York, NY: St. Martin's Press, 1996. A lyrical natural history of a New England swamp, focusing on the lives of spotted turtles and illustrated with the author's own excellent artwork.

Field Guides

Reptiles and Amphibians of Eastern and Central North America, by Roger Conant and Joseph T. Collins. Boston, MA: Houghton Mifflin, 1998. This classic guidebook has been updated to include the most recent taxonomic revisions.

Local field guides have been published for reptiles and amphibians in many states and regions. A visit to a university or large city library or an online search should reveal titles covering your area.

Useful Websites

Center for North American Herpetology
www.cnah.org

The Center for North American Herpetology promotes education about and conservation of reptiles and amphibians. The website includes links to a variety of turtle-related websites and herpetology atlases as well as state, regional, and national herpetological societies.

Chelonian Conservation and Biology
www.chelonian.org

This organization publishes the *International Journal of Turtle and Tortoise Research,* as well as an online newsletter that includes articles about North American turtles.

Desert Tortoise Council
www.deserttortoise.org
   This nonprofit group works to assure the continued survival of the desert tortoise throughout its range. Its website includes an online newsletter and announcements of meetings, workshops, and symposia.

Gopher Tortoise Council
www.gophertortoisecouncil.org
   Formed by a group of scientists, the Gopher Tortoise Council is working to prevent the rangewide decline of the gopher tortoise.

Gopher Tortoise Organization
www.gophertortoise.org
   This nonprofit group focuses on gopher tortoise conservation and education in Florida.

Home of the Map Turtles
www.graptemys.com
   Information on all species and subspecies of map turtles in North America.

Kingsnake Club
www.kingsnake.com
   Here you can access an online pet and wild animal shelter and rescue network providing adoption and placement for reptiles and amphibians.

Western Pond Turtle Project
www.pondturtle.com
   The story of a successful project to help restore the western pond turtle to the state of Washington.

Wood Turtle
www.woodturtle.com
   Set up by Canadian turtle scientist Raymond Saumure, this website seeks to promote the conservation of the wood turtle through education and research.

Major Herpetological Societies

Three North American societies are devoted to herpetology. They all welcome members from the general public as well as academia. These groups publish journals describing scientific research on turtles; the journals can be found in university libraries. In addition to these three major organizations, many states and local regions also have herpetological societies.

American Society of Ichthyologists and Herpetologists (www.asih.org) publishes *Copeia*.

Herpetologists' League (www.inhs.uiuc.edu/cbd/HL/HL.html) publishes *Herpetologica* and *Herpetological Monographs*.

The Society for the Study of Amphibians and Reptiles (www.ssarherps.org) publishes *Herpetological Review, Journal of Herpetology,* and *Catalogue of American Amphibians and Reptiles*.

Also available in Stackpole's Wild Guide series

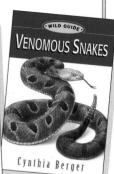

BEARS
Charles Fergus

$19.95 • 128 pages • 22 color photos • 15 color illustrations
978-0-8117-3251-2

DRAGONFLIES
Cynthia Berger

$19.95 • 136 pages • 60 color illustrations
978-0-8117-2971-0

OWLS
Cynthia Berger

$19.95 • 144 pages • 30 color photos • 22 color illustrations
978-0-8117-3213-0

VENOMOUS SNAKES
Cynthia Berger

$19.95 • 120 pages • 26 color photos • 10 color illustrations
978-0-8117-3412-7

WWW.STACKPOLEBOOKS.COM
1-800-732-3669